ATTACK OF THE KILLER VIDEO BOOK

TIPS AND TRICKS FOR YOUNG DIRECTORS

ATTACK OF THE KILLER VIDEO BOOK

TIPS AND TRICKS FOR YOUNG DIRECTORS

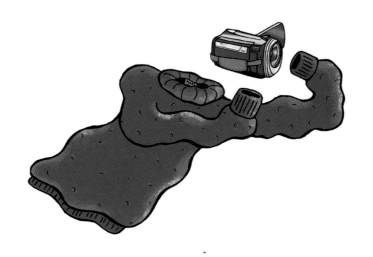

REVISED AND UPDATED EDITION

BY MARK SHULMAN AND HAZLITT KROG

ART BY MARTHA NEWBIGGING

annick press
toronto + new york + vancouver

Designed by Sheryl Shapiro

Annick Press Ltd.

We acknowledge the support of the Canada Council for the Arts, the Ontario Arts Council, and the Government of Canada through the Canada Book Fund (CBF) for our publishing activities.

The publisher wishes to thank Colin Foster of Big Woo Films and Philip Hoffman of the York University Department of Film & Video for looking over the manuscript.

ONTARIO ARTS COUNCIL
CONSEIL DES ARTS DE L'ONTARIO

Cataloging in Publication

Shulman, Mark
    Attack of the killer video book take 2 : tips & tricks for young directors / by Mark Shulman and Hazlitt Krog ; art by Martha Newbigging. — Rev and updated ed.

Includes index.
ISBN 978-1-55451-367-3 (bound).—ISBN 978-1-55451-366-6 (pbk.)

    1. Video recordings—Production and direction—Juvenile literature. I. Krog, Hazlitt II. Newbigging, Martha III. Title.

PN1992.94.S48 2012   j778.59   C2011-907229-7

Distributed in Canada by:
Firefly Books Ltd.
66 Leek Crescent
Richmond Hill, ON
L4B 1H1

Published in the U.S.A. by Annick Press (U.S.) Ltd.
Distributed in the U.S.A. by:
Firefly Books (U.S.) Inc.
P.O. Box 1338
Ellicott Station
Buffalo, NY 14205

Printed in China

The art in this book was hand-drawn, scanned, and then colored in Photoshop.

Visit us at: www.annickpress.com
Visit Mark Shulman at: www.Shul.mn
Visit Hazlitt Krog at: www.hazlitt.com
Visit Martha Newbigging at: www.marthanewbigging.com

To my father, who always held the camera and left few pictures of himself.

To my children, whose father seems to be doing the same thing.

—M.S.

To every kid who ever hit *record* and was hooked.

—H.K.

To Rose and Eugene, who taught me the magic of animation.

—M.N.

ACKNOWLEDGMENTS

For Ethan and Tali Beckwith-Cohen; Anders and Celia Bottger; Rachel Chazanoff; Amalya and Aidan Cleland; Isabel and Lila Count; Sophie, Lily, and Abby Edelman; Cormac and Lucy Farley; Emma and Chloe Friedman; Isabella Gallicchio; Nina and Bruno Harris; Paladin Lamison; Remo Marcaccio; Isaac and Clara Moss; Liza Rae, Lucy, and Charlie Rolander; and all the other future visionaries: We want good stories filled with interesting people. Thank you, thank you, to Hazlitt Krog, for friendship, perseverance, and for sharing his many talents. Huge thanks to professors Ken Wilson and Joseph DeRoller of East High School in Rochester, N.Y., for explaining movies so enjoyably. And thanks to George Eastman, inventor of Kodak film in my hometown. Without him, we'd all be going to a lot more plays.

—Mark Shulman

I'd like to acknowledge a few of the many wonderful people who have inspired and assisted me on my path to completing this book: Dzogchen Khenpo Choga Rinpoche, Tina Krog, Alexia Moore, Gina Olmedo, Dr. William Jungels, Bob Kovacs, and all my Dharma friends and family members. Special thanks to my co-author, Mark, a prolific creative genius who has remained my true friend through thick and thin and especially through rewrites. A very special thanks to Dr. Norman and Helen Krog, who gave me more than I'll ever know, including my start in this world. They also gave me many amazing gifts: a movie camera, movie projector, still camera, darkroom, computer, car, guitar, and, by encouraging me to ask questions, the boundless enthusiasm to be an explorer.

—Hazlitt Krog

Make Fun!
Make Friends!
Make Trouble!
Make a Million Dollars!
Make Videos!

Even if you don't make a million dollars right away, you can make outrageously good videos. All you need is a little creativity, some patience, lots of light, and this book.*

If you want to say something, see something, or save an experience forever, video is the way to go. You can create entertainment or an audiovisual diary. You can practice being a director, writer, actor, singer, or interviewer. And believe it or not, five or ten years later, you'll be happy to see what you looked like at this age. Whatever you choose to do in the age of video, understanding the art and science today can help you take a starring role tomorrow.

You are very wise indeed to be reading this book. We have packed hundreds of tons of useful information and helpful hints into just 76 pages (not including the front and back covers). In fact, by the time you are finished with *this one page*, you will know more than when you began.

Most important, keep your eyes open when you're watching a professional video. Everything you learn here you'll be able to see in the work of the pros. The pros are your best teachers.

The info in this book is a good start. We'll give you the basics, from thinking to planning to shooting to editing, without being scary. And then we'll let you loose on the world. Every videomaker has a story to tell. Just press the REC button, and tell it.

Moves to make before making your movie

Try this simple exercise. Look in the mirror and ask yourself, "Am I a brilliant video master with 'Hollywood Legend' written all over my face?" Now move that face up and down. The answer is "Yes."

*And a video camera.

ROAD MAP

Y ou don't need a lot of money, or experience, or famous friends. Follow this simple route to success.

HEAD

The Inspiration

10

When video ideas come in a brainstorm, it's customary to shout "Eureka!" (a brand of vacuum cleaner). Some people shout "Hoover!" or "Electrolux!" but it still means you've got a great idea for your video, and that's the first step.

Full Team Ahead

13

Don't be a maniac; moviemaking is a team sport. It's more fun to share the details of planning, scripting, shooting, and editing. Let others have input, or they'll leave you holding the camera bag.

The Story

15

Remember screaming about vacuum cleaners? Grab a pen and put that brilliant brainstorm on paper. This helps you keep focused when the craziness of shooting starts, and it gives your team a goal to remember. Don't forget this – there's a quiz later: *Every video tells a story, and everything in the video should help tell the story.* Your video may need a script or a visual storyboard or just a loose set of notes. Without a script, you'll be shooting from the hip and probably miss your target. There are simple tricks to telling a story on video, and learning them will keep your audience coming back for more.

Planning

Pre-production is Hollywood lingo for "planning before you get in too deep." First talk with your team and make some decisions about the equipment, costumes, locations, and more. Figure out the *locations* where you're going to shoot. Make a list of the *props* (the parachute, the sword) and *costumes* (the fake nose, the Viking helmet) you're using. Make sure everyone brings what they need — or promised to bring — before shooting starts. Write down your shooting schedule. It sounds like homework, but that's only because it *is* homework.

The Technology

Want to know what it takes to get rolling right away? Having a camera's a good start. Buy, beg, or borrow, but don't steal one. You won't need the latest and greatest. Even an old tape-based camera can do the job nicely if you can get the matching blank tapes and get the videotape converted into files on your hard drive. With just a few more essentials, you can get your shoot started.

The Technique

Do yourself a favor. Do your audience a favor. Learn the basics of holding a camera, moving a camera, zooming the lens, controlling the sound, controlling the light, and controlling your stomach when it starts grumbling. You won't believe the difference a little learning will make.

The Special Effects

You may not have the *Star Wars* budget of George Lucas, but you can have his imagination. With real-time visual effects, sound effects, and camera tricks, you'll shock and amaze everyone. Especially yourself.

The Burden of Leadership

Remember the days when directors screamed through megaphones and carried little whips? Neither do we. Camera skills and writing skills are important, but directing is also about people skills. Use them (the skills) or lose them (the people).

Post-Production

Once you've captured everything you need, you're mostly done. Now comes the polishing part. Final editing helps the pieces come together. Adding music, titles, and other effects will help make your mild-mannered movie a marvelous masterpiece all ready to be uploaded and applauded.

The Big Show

Premiere means "first," so be sure your first show is first class. Make invitations. Make posters. Make popcorn. Make them be quiet. You've put a lot of time into your video. Keep them in their seats without using glue.

YOUR OSCAR-NIGHT SPEECH
Run up to the stage. Cry a lot. Say something political with your fist in the air. Remember to thank "the little people" who made your success possible. Then run like the wind as you're chased down the street by little people.

COOL!

Thinking in Video

Let's get a couple of things straight. First of all, this book is going to use the words *video* and *movie* to mean the same thing. Even if your video isn't a movie, it's boring to read the word *video, video, video* over and over and over. So, whatever you make will be a video *and* a movie.

Next thing to know is that a video is really a lot of still pictures (*frames*) seen in a fast sequence. How fast? Try 30 frames per second, 1,800 frames per minute, 108,000 frames per hour. When you're done watching a three-hour movie about can openers, you've seen 324,000 single images. That's a lot of can openers. No wonder you're hungry.

Video camera or still camera

Dare we compare? Lighting and composition (setting up your shot) are similar. But still cameras get blurry when you move too quickly ... and video cameras make the viewer feel blurry when you move too quickly.

Since a video is lots of still images, can you get action from still pictures? You bet – in fact, that's how it all started. The earliest motion pictures were flip books, a stack of drawings or photos with each image just a little different from the one before it. Riff the stack with your thumb and *presto!* Action without lights or camera. Page 19 will tell you more.

But it's easier to use a video camera: your talent won't have to play "freeze tag" with your still camera, and you won't have to draw lots of little running stick figures for your flip book.

You are always telling a story

Here's another word you'll see a lot here: *story*. Remember that you are always, always telling a story with your video camera. Every second of your video has to help tell that story, or else it doesn't belong. Your audience will be (a) bored or (b) confused or (c) both. Keep your story in mind every moment you shoot. It's the second-oldest rule in movies (after "use a camera").

What's that? You think you don't know how to tell stories with video? Sure you do. You've probably seen so many

movies, TV shows, music videos, and commercials that you know the basic rules of visual storytelling without even realizing it. (See "What You See is What They Get" on page 30 for more clues.)

Some basic rules of visual storytelling

- What is happening? What do you want your viewer to do? Laugh? Cry? Scream? Be impressed with you? Always think about what your audience is thinking.
- Everything you shoot is a choice. Are you making choices that make sense for your particular video? Do they match the feeling you're trying to get?
- *Are you telling the story?* Are the characters, words, actions, settings, props, and effects helping tell the story, in big or little ways?
- Pay attention to the *frame* (the borders of the rectangle that will be the edges of your video). Everything should enter, exit, or stay in the frame for a reason.
- Whatever you're shooting is your *subject*. It can be a person or a tree. The viewer should always know who or what the subject of your video is.
- Movies are about something *happening*. And something has to move – your subject or your camera. Storytelling is action.
- Move the camera slooooowly when you move it. (Lots more on that later.)

That's just the beginning, but it's a good start. Now that you know a few rules, it's time to start thinking about the video YOU want to shoot.

What's the Big Idea?

If someone asks what your video's about, your answer is called the *concept*. If you can describe it in one sentence, that's the concept. *Darth Vader meets Godzilla* is a concept. So is *Batman's mom cleans the Bat Cave and throws out his comic books*. And so is *Two girl detectives discover their friend is a spy*. What more can we say? Write your movie's concept before going to the next step.

Concept-O-Matic™

It's easy to do! You can, too!
"My video is about what happens when …"

Start with a story:
Owen is cut from the team.

Add props: Owen breaks his leg.

Add characters:
Owen sits out football practice.

Add setting:
Owen sits out the big game.

Choices, choices

What you shoot depends a lot on what you have available. Are you interested in exploring the real world or in making up worlds of your own? Think about the story you want to tell and a feeling you want to share. Or do you just like acting silly in front of the camera?

Fake Out

Fictional Video Ideas

SHORT STORIES
Plan ahead. Shoot with a script. Keep it short.

IMPROVISED
No script. Stories and comedy made up on the fly.

TV SHOWS
Talk shows, game shows, or imitate your favorite show.

MUSIC VIDEOS
Sing a song or sing along.

MASH-UPS
Find some audio and video, mix it up, and make it your own.

FAKE COMMERCIALS
Make fun of ads. If it smells, it sells.

EXPERIMENTAL FILMS
Usually more fun to make than to watch.

Get Real

Documentary Video Ideas

A SIMPLE PROCESS
A great place to get started. (see pages 14–15)

BIOGRAPHY
Interview someone you know, or someone you don't.

NEWS
Something happened, let's investigate the stories.

SCHOOL
Sports, clubs, events, a year-end video yearbook.

EVENTS
Parties, parades, plays, practical jokes, etc.

REALITY TV
The actual adventures of you and your friends.

NATURE
Fluffy's amazing pet tricks. Or cheese getting moldy.

VIDEO BLOG/VLOG
A moving diary. You, your life, your rants, even your summer vacation.

FULL TEAM AHEAD

So you're the director. In Hollywood, directors make the decisions because they're the experts. At your house, you're the director because you've got the camera. But that's no reason to hog all the fun. If you don't let the other kids share the pleasure, you'll end up videoing the flowers out back. All alone.

Like most of us, you probably have one or three friends to shoot with. That means people will be doing double duty behind the camera (*crew*) and in front of the camera (*talent*). Since everyone can't hold the camera, you'd better know what other jobs to offer instead.

One Live Crew

Here's a list of essential roles for making a video. Sometimes just a few people do everything. And if you're going to do everything, you might as well find out your official titles.

WRITER – in charge of the story and dialog

DIRECTOR – the visionary who controls and manages the movie's creation

CAMERA OPERATOR – sets up, operates, and deals with the camera

SOUND PERSON – deals with all aspects of microphones and capturing sound

GAFFER – in charge of electricity, lighting, and taping cords down

GRIP – in charge of the sets and props; sometimes helps with the camera

STYLIST – in charge of costumes, makeup, actors' props

TALENT – those who work in front of the camera

EXTRA – a background actor who fills space around main actors

EFFECTS – creates and executes the special effects

EDITOR – puts all the pieces together at the end

PRODUCER – supervisor, also known as "a responsible adult"

CATERER – see Producer

TRANSPORTATION – see Producer

EXECUTIVE PRODUCER – a producer who provides funds or very good food

STUDIO CHIEF – the owner of the video gear

GOING SOLO

What's that? Your crew is busy doing homework? Relax, Hitchcock ... solo projects don't have to make you psycho:

Keep it simple. Don't bite off more than you can shoot.

Plan ahead. Plan ahead. Plan ahead. Plan ahead.

Travel light. All you really need is a camera, some blank media (i.e., memory cards or tapes), charged batteries, a charger (just in case), a camera bag to keep things safe, and a shot list in case you want to know what you're doing.

Nonfiction videos especially lend themselves to solo shooting: interviews, events, and nature videos.

If you've got fiction on your mind, puppets, dolls, and hands make surprisingly well-behaved actors. You'll have to do the talking, though. Or, set up the camera somewhere stable and strut your stuff onscreen.

The Talent

Who's the biggest ham on camera? The actors are called talent, but that's no guarantee of actual talent.

Casting means choosing the right actor for each part. If there are only two of you, it also helps to be a master of disguise. If your video has a script, encourage your actors to memorize their lines before the shoot. It's all right if they change their lines if the changes make sense for the movie.

Enough Reading! Let's Make a Video!

Ready? Get set ... grab your camera! Get a memory card that fits in the slot. Find the red REC button. Aim the camera at something. Sooner or later hit the REC button again to stop recording. Grab the right cable and figure out how to get the files to play back on your computer. Kick back and watch. Cool, huh?

Go ahead and satisfy that itchy recording finger. Let practice make perfect, then come back to the book for your next steps up the video ladder.

GET ROLLING!

Becoming a powerful director requires exercise. Here's an exercise. It may not be *Planet of the Grapes*, but it's a start.

Record a *simple process*. A what? Here are some examples:

- making a sandwich
- mowing the lawn
- washing the dog
- giving a wet dog a sandwich on the lawn

As the director/cameraperson, pretend you are invisible. Just let the action happen on its own, so it seems as natural as possible. You can let the camera stay in one place or try close-ups, wide shots, and different angles to help tell your story.

The simpler and shorter the process, the better. Here's what you can accidentally learn by making simple-process videos:

First Steps in Planning

Have a brainstorming party: Get your people together to share ideas.

Agree on what's possible: Don't try to do what you can't do. Without a parachute, you can't get that aerial zoom shot you want. If you don't own the camera, forget the scuba-diving movie. But if you're not trying to damage the equipment or yourself, a lot of choices await you.

Add up equipment and resources:

- What brains and muscle are available?
- What gear can you get?
- Are extra lights necessary?
- Do you have enough gaffer's tape (a.k.a. duct tape)?
- What can you build?
- What can you borrow?
- What do you need to buy?
- What can replace the thing you don't have, so you can still tell your story?

TIP

Everybody has an idea. You should listen to them all, no matter how stupid they seem at first. (Or, if you're going solo, don't argue with yourself.)

- how to show the individual steps of doing something
- how to capture a series of nice-looking shots
- how to match one shot to the next so it all fits together and looks right in the end
- how to work with talent (even hungry, wet dogs)

When you are done, you will have told a short story on video. It will probably be only a minute or two long. Later on, we'll get into the details of storytelling. For now, just get the feeling. Then plug it in, watch the results, and decide what you'll do differently, or the same, next time. The best learning is by doing.

Ready for more? Then power down the camera and read up.

From Brainstorm to Story

Writing for video is not so scary when you go step by step. One writing tool you might not have thought about is ... the video camera. Turn it on and point it at people. Use it as a rehearsal monitor. Work out your story ideas. Work out the main parts of the movie: plot, settings, characters. Try out some dialog. Then play back your recordings to get ideas for your storyboard or script. If it works, keep it. First stop: the plot.

The plot

In the beginning, there was the one-sentence concept. The *plot* is the next step – a little longer, but equally important. It's the description of what's happening, and what's at stake for the characters. A plot may take a full minute to describe while a concept takes five seconds. Write out your plot as a short story of a few paragraphs, until it's a story you can get excited about.

The setting

The setting is where the video takes place. It could be a bedroom or a planet, depending on your story. (Or both.) It could be in the year 1967 or 94965. Your imagination is the only limitation. A short movie might have only one setting, but longer movies almost always have more. If the setting is at night, try to make sure the sun doesn't peek through a window. See "Location, Location, Location" on page 20 for a little more encouragement here.

The characters

Your characters are the people in your story. Maybe they're real, maybe they're *a little like* people you know, maybe they're fungus monsters from the earth's core. That's up to you. In every story, we want to know about and care about what happens to the characters. Every character's story should have a beginning (they rise out of the ocean), a middle (they tear apart your bedroom. "Honest, Mom, it wasn't me!"), and an end (your mother tells you to put down that camera and do your homework).

Even if their stories are not the most important, make sure they do something memorable. Your video will be as interesting as its characters. Think about how many movies have left you thinking, "Who cares about those people?" That is, if you care to think about them at all.

In a documentary, the talent are real people with real stories. But what happens to them will be just as interesting if you let their stories come out naturally. Don't push … coax! If you let your real-life characters be natural, they may not look like they're selling cola on TV, but they'll be much more interesting.

The dialog

"Hey, you!" "Me?" "Yeah, you!" "What do you want?" "What do I want??" "Yeah." "Um, I don't remember. Forget it." "I already did."

Welcome to the world of dialog. Dialog is the conversation between characters in your story. It's the place where they tell you things about themselves, and the audience learns what's going on in the story. Think about your characters and what makes them tick. Get inside their heads. What would they say in the imaginary situations you put them in?

The script

If you're comfortable with the idea of writing a script for your story, it doesn't have to be hard. Most scripts have all the things you just read about – setting, characters, dialog – plus details like sound effects and camera angles. But mainly it will have the dialog. There's an example on page 67.

If you're not ready to sit and write it all down, maybe you'd be happier making a storyboard. Yeah, a storyboard. Hey, what's a storyboard?

The Storyboard
What's a storyboard?

Glad you asked. The storyboard is a tool the movie director and crew use to imagine how the movie will look *before* it is made.

A storyboard looks a lot like a comic book. Each square is a drawing that shows you what the camera will see, from the moment the director yells "Action!" until the director yells "Cut!" In the next square, which would normally be a new camera set-up, you visualize the change of camera angle and position, and the action continues. Sometimes in one minute there will be several shots (and therefore several drawings). Other times the camera might not move for a minute or more, so you'd only need one drawing to represent it.

Next to each drawing you place the matching dialog words, as well as camera set-up and production notes to help you and your crew visualize what the camera will do, what will happen onscreen, and what you will hear on the soundtrack.

"Hey, you!"
"Me?"
"Yeah, you!"
"What do you want?"
"What do I want?"
"Forget it."
"I already did."

TIP

The less talking you have, the better your actors will look! Actions speak louder than words anyway. Definitely don't use the actors to explain the plot: "Mom, remember when I had a secret map and I buried it under the garage so the zombie dude next door wouldn't find the family treasure that Grandpa hid after he invented the giant robot? Well, I lost it." You might as well have your actor sing a lullaby; your audience is fast asleep.

Why you need to make a storyboard

- Lets you see the film better in your mind, so you can fix problems before shooting starts

- Helps you figure out the best camera angles

- Helps you be prepared before and during the shooting

- Helps you get away without writing a script

- Helps you show off your best stick figures

How to make a storyboard

Let's say you're filming a movie called *The Incredible Killer Sweater from Outer Space*. Here are the steps to making your own storyboard:

Draw a page with four boxes on it.

Label the boxes *Shot 1*, *Shot 2*, *Shot 3*, and *Shot 4*.

The first box is your first shot of the movie, **Shot 1**. It is a medium shot (see pages 31–34 for shot types) of a sweater flying through the air and landing on a chair. You can't see who threw it. Write next to the box, *Add ominous swooshing sound effect as sweater flies through air.*

In the box for **Shot 2** you draw a person walking into the room from a wide angle. Next to the box write, *Footsteps can be heard as Bernie enters the room from left side of screen.*

In **Shot 3** you draw the person finding the sweater from a medium shot. Next to the box write, *Bernie wonders out loud, "Now how did this sweater get over here?"*

In **Shot 4** you draw the person putting on the sweater using a close-up on their head and shoulders. Next to the box write, *Add scary music in the soundtrack.*

Of course, on the next page you'll have four more boxes. That's where Bernie struggles with the alien sweater monster. Then you show him crushed by the sweater and lying dead on the floor. Dead Bernie is next to the sweater. Then the sweater (tied to invisible fishing line) is pulled across the floor off camera.

You see? Making a killer storyboard is no sweat.

WHAT? I CAN MAKE A MOVIE WITHOUT A VIDEO CAMERA?

If you're not using a dedicated video camera but you have a computer, some technical knowledge, and maybe a still camera or webcam, you can make movies. What's the benefit? Most still cameras take better still photos than what you can capture on most video cameras. Your final files will probably be smaller, too – easier to e-mail and upload.

Plan: Come up with a simple concept. Make a storyboard. Number each shot. Write a short script if there's any talking.

Collect: Open a folder in your computer to collect the images you need for your story. Where are the images coming from?

SAY CHEESE: Take a series of still photos or video clips of your actors doing each action that helps tell the story. If you used a digital still camera, transfer the files to your hard drive. If you used a webcam, the stills or video clips will be saved directly to your hard drive.

NO CAMERA? Use existing photos, magazine pages, drawings, or anything else, and scan them into your computer.

NO SCANNER? Use a simple drawing or painting program to whip up the images you want for your story. Now they're ready to go.

Borrow: For school projects, using images you find online is normally considered fair use (check with your teacher first). Download the images, but always give credit where credit is due.

Speak: Most computers have a microphone, or a jack for one. Many cell phones double as digital voice recorders, too. You (and any actors) can record lines of dialog, then save them onto your hard drive as a series of audio files.

Cleanup: Select dialog files you want to keep. Edit your photos or storyboard images. You can crop, change colors, or add cool special effects.

Hey! We recommend you get help from an adult for the next steps. Go to page 53 for more.

Install: Go find a computer with video editing software. You can even use presentation software (like PowerPoint or Keynote) to put a movie together. If that's not available, ask the computer's owner to download and install some demo or freeware video editing software (see page 54 for suggestions).

GET PERMISSION TO DOWNLOAD IF IT'S NOT YOUR COMPUTER.

Import: Import the edited dialog and images into the video editing software. You can also add music along with the dialog.

Edit: Sound goes first. With the editing software, arrange all the sound elements (dialog, narration, and music) in a *timeline* (in order) until you're happy. Then arrange the visual images in your editing timeline to match up with the soundtrack. View and listen, tweak and twack, until you have a movie you are proud of.

Output: When you're done editing, *render* your masterpiece (page 56) to a finished video file. You can upload it to a video sharing site, post it on your website, or burn a DVD. All this with no video camera!

Professional moviemakers use this technique to explore a movie idea before they shoot it. It's called an *animatic*, which is basically a storyboard on video with a soundtrack. All big-budget special effects features start out as animatics.

PLANNING

They Call It Pre-production

Pre-production is the official name. Planning's the game. Once you've figured out your story, you'll save a lot of time with a little planning. And believe us, moviemaking takes plenty of time. (You think this is all going to happen one day after school? Two words: For Getit.) Doing it right means taking your time (maybe days, maybe a week or more) and respecting your team's time. Planning makes it all go more smoothly.

The more you plan, the happier your team will be at the end of the shoot, and the better your movie will turn out. It's been proven about a million times.

Or ignore this advice and grab the camera and go wild. Your choice.

Location, Location, Location

Which came first – the ghost story about the floating head or the spooky house to shoot it in? That house is the location of your video. If you live in a house that inspires floating-head stories, that's your problem. If you don't, your problem is called location scouting. You have to find the creepy house, find the (possibly) creepy owners, and, creepiest of all … gasp! … get permission.

Make your life easy: Shoot in locations where you can easily get permission. Choose your locations based on your story, but also base your story around the locations that are easy to work in. It's better to change a few ideas than to send the entire crew to Mount Everest to bring your vision to life.

Props and Costumes

The story calls for a mean sheriff, a brave cowgirl, and the three-legged dog who saves her. Where are you going to get them?

Okay, your Aunt Greta has the western hats and the boots. Actors' clothes are called *costumes*.

Your cousin Vidalia has the rope and the toy gun. *Props* are all the things you see on camera that actors use or need. A phone, a coffee cup, a laser-guided missile launcher – these are all props.

But forget turning the neighborhood dog into "Hopalong."

HMMM... HOW ABOUT A PIRATE ADVENTURE SET ON AUNT BETTY'S SAILBOAT?

HOW TO MAKE HERE LOOK LIKE THERE

Some suggestions to jump-start your imagination (and annoy the principal). Creative camera angles can really fool the eye.

School cafeteria = prison cafeteria
Furnace room = 1950s space station
Sandy beach = the vast Sahara
Nurse's office = hospital room
Principal's office = torture chamber
Garage or basement = mad scientist's lair
Old buildings = the past
New buildings = the future
Tree house = secret fortress
Lawn (super close up) = the jungle
Toilet (super super close up) = the ocean

Prop up your budget

You can avoid buying props and costumes by (1) asking people to donate them and (2) making a movie that only uses things people already own. Why bother shopping? Make a list of all the things people promised to bring. Remind them the day before. This way, they might actually bring what you need to the shoot.

Be creative and improvise with what you find at home. Look in your attic or closets for old family clothes from a bygone era of 10 or 100 years ago. If you can't find or borrow everything you need, try tag sales/garage sales and thrift stores. Stay away from expensive items and Dumpsters.

Working backwards

Finding old clothes and props could inspire your whole movie. Thin ties? Jackets without collars? Whoa — the 1980s! Can you believe what they wore in the days before DVDs? You've got a time-machine story there. Get writing!

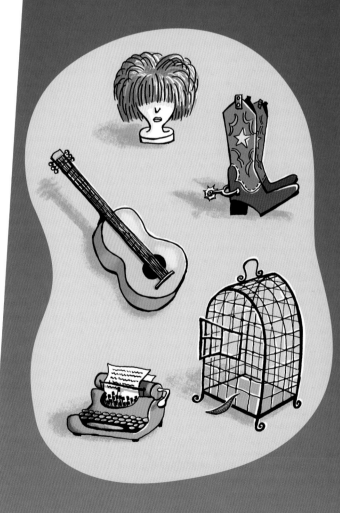

Camera!!!

And now, believe it or not, we're actually going to pick up the camera.

Don't be intimidated by your camera. Manufacturers sometimes put tons of features into cameras to make you feel like you're getting a lot for your money. And they change those features every year so you'll buy a new one. But the most important features are the same on every camera, and those features are the ones to really know and use. Explore the menus and get familiar with what all those funny words mean.

If you ever get lost navigating your way around all the buttons, knobs, and menus, remember *RTM – Read The Manual*. Your camera manual is filled with great technical secrets, and some not-so-secret things. It can help you figure out most of your questions without having to run to some adult who didn't read the manual either. And you can download it for free on the manufacturer's site, so you'll never lose it.

Everything's a video camera?

If you don't have a video camera, or if you need a better one, you have a few options beyond hitting up your parents.

Ask teachers, parents, friends, parents of friends, friends of parents. Shop at thrift stores and online auction sites. Follow your local TV news van and when they're done covering the fire, say, "Can I have that camera?" No, wait, don't say that. Say, "May I?"

Camera Don'ts and Don'ts

Don't forget to get permission to use it.
Don't drop it.
Don't get it wet.
Don't pick it up by the tripod or use it to open walnuts.
Don't touch it with dirty, greasy, foody hands.
Don't swing it around in a china shop.
Don't leave it unattended near crooks and bad guys.
Don't do anything else dumb.
Don't.

TIP

Pick a resolution. Then find out how long you can record on your camera's media by pointing the camera at a clock. Run it until the memory is full. Now you know.

Which cam will you cord with?

Camcorder PRO

Usually highest quality; more features, including optical (in-the-lens) zoom; audio input jacks for microphones; larger display; can shoot for hours; tripod mount.

Camcorder CON

More expensive compared to most of the other choices; only does one job (though it does it best).

Still camera or cell phone PRO

Good for shooting conversations, one-take videos, news reporting; easy to switch from still photo to movie mode; uploads easily to computer or sharing sites; phone is always with you so you can shoot from the hip.

Still camera or cell phone CON

Not always good-quality video; poor sound quality on long shots; phone has limited storage, no optical zoom, and no mount for tripod to hold it still.

Webcam (built-in or connected to computer) PRO

No need to transfer video – it's already in the computer, ready for playback and editing; built-in "tripod."

Webcam CON

REALLY not portable; clunky compared to a real hand-held camera; poor sound quality on long shots; no optical zoom; easy to drop on foot.

Tablet PRO

Shoot and edit right in the device (such as with iMovie on the iPad); bigger screen makes it a better playback device than a phone.

Tablet CON

Poor sound quality on long shots; awkward shape to hold; no tripod mount; no optical zoom; fragile.

Camera resolutions

Most digital cameras let you shoot higher resolution (better quality, but bigger files) or lower resolution (smaller files, but lower quality). Your camera probably has a few of these choices.

■ Jump up one level in this chart = your video will use up your hard drive faster + slower editing + slower rendering.
■ For your practice movies, working at 480p will make your computer faster. Go above 720p when you've got the patience to make it shine.

Resolution	How Many Horizontal Pixels (width of screen)		How Many Vertical Pixels (height of screen)	(W)idescreen or (S)tandard Aspect Ratio
Higher Quality				
4K (Ultra HD)	4096	x	2304	16:9 (W)
1080p (Full HD)	1920	x	1080	16:9 (W)
720p (HD = High Def)	1280	x	720	16:9 (W)
480p (Wide VGA)	854	x	480	16:9 (W)
480p (VGA)	640	x	480	4:3 (S)
360p (Low Def TV)	480	x	360	4:3 (S)
240p (Quarter VGA) **Smallest files**	320	x	240	4:3 (S)

HAS ANYONE SEEN THE BATTERY CHARGER?

Everything You Need to Know About Using the Camera

Shooting video is not too difficult – IF you don't push any buttons that you're not sure of. RTM if you get stuck. Here are the key concepts:

Feel the power

Make sure the batteries are full of juice, including your spare. Now turn on the camera.

Get set

All video cameras let you choose between record mode and playback mode. Depending on your model, *record* may also be called *REC*, *camera*, or *movie* mode. *Playback* is sometimes called *play* or – on old tape cameras – *VCR* mode. When the switch is set to *record*, you'll be recording as soon as you press the red REC button, which should be under your thumb.

Get carded

Does your camera use a memory card to store video? Get an extra memory card. You won't have to interrupt your shoot to download files.

Before you start your shoot, make sure all the important files on the card have been downloaded correctly. Once you double check, you can format and reuse the card.

Tape it

If you're using an ancient camcorder you found in a time capsule, it may require something called "tapes." They're little plastic cassettes filled with spools of tape used to capture your video footage. Don't confuse it with the sticky "tape" that holds your posters to the wall.

Without getting too technical, if you don't put a tape in your camcorder, the cam won't cord. There were a number of competing tape formats back in the day. Each one claimed it was the best. We can tell you the truth: The best tape format is the one that fits your camcorder. Finding blank tapes may require opening another time capsule, winning an auction, or visiting a thrift store.

Tape could be a showstopper! Getting from videotape to hard drive requires: a special cable, a special device, or a professional service.

CAN YOU SAY CCD?

Now that film and videotape are as common as dial phones, what exactly is capturing your digital image? The CCD (Charge-Coupled Device). Its job? To be a sensor that converts light into digital ones and zeros. Its size? A postage stamp, yet it's covered with millions of tiny dots called pixels. (One million pixels is a megapixel.) Its trick? To catch the image coming from the lens so each tiny pixel knows exactly what color or shade to be. When you zoom in to your picture, the dots you see are pixels up close. The CCD converts the pixels and delivers them into digital files that you call photos and movies. Remember, your movie camera's CCD is recording and delivering 30 images per second, which makes you look like a slacker.

Re-media education

It's always better to use blank media and have some spares on hand in case you run out. But if you must recycle, make sure you aren't recording over Aunt Eileen's kidney surgery video (unless that's what you want). Use playback mode to view your media first. If you'd rather not take the risk of erasing something, transfer the precious video to your computer, or burn it on a DVD. Delete or erase the old video from your media, then switch back to record mode when you are ready to start recording a new segment.

Insta-Light

If your camera comes with a built-in light, the good news is that you won't always need extra lighting. The bad news: It will drink your battery dry. Bring a spare, and use the light wisely. More about lighting later (see pages 35–39).

Sound thinking

Your camera's built-in microphone isn't meant for long distances, loud places, or windy days. (It's also not meant for spreading peanut butter on rye bread.) If you're doing a simple shoot with nearby talent in a somewhat quiet place, your camera's mic will do the job. Otherwise you might want to think about an extension or wireless mic. We'll explain that later, too (see pages 40–41).

Take aim

Point the camera at your victim. Most video cameras have automatic focus (keeping the blur away), automatic exposure (deciding how much light you need), and stabilization (reducing your jitters), so you don't have to worry about setting them yourself. RTM for more details.

Shoot

Press the record button to start recording. Press it again to stop recording. You captured your shot.

Okay. Those are the basic basics. Now what?

STORAGE FORMATS

No fooling, here are a few of the many consumer video storage options you might run across in your search for a new or used video camera:

Built-In
Hard Drive (used in many digital camcorders)
Flash Memory (used in many pocket video cameras)
Removable Card Memory (mostly Flash RAM)
Secure Digital (SD cards in various physical sizes)
Memory Stick (various physical card sizes)
CompactFlash (includes Microdrive)
Cassette Tape
DV Digital Video (MiniDV, DVCPRO)
VHS (VHS-C, S-VHS)
8mm Video (Video8, Hi-8, Digital8)
Betamax (long defunct, but still cool)

… and probably 40 other letter/ number combinations, most of which are either rusting on the ash heap of video history or were not yet invented when this book was published. By the time you read this, three formats will be off the list and five more will be on it.

Remember, the most important media is the one that fits your camera. Don't fret that you lack the latest and greatest. The differences aren't that important. It's all about what you do with what you have now.

Great Idea

Practice makes perfect

Record some practice shots with your camera and play them back. Then play your favorite movie and watch for tilting, panning, and other motion shots to see how your camerawork compares.

Use a dolly for tracking shots

Great Idea

When you want the camera to move a distance (say, while people walk and talk), you need a dolly. A baby's dolly gets pushed in a carriage. A professional dolly is like a railroad track. You push the camera along the rails on a cart. Instead of building a railroad, here's something just as good for rolling that camera along.

Dolly 1 Borrow a wheelchair or a chair on wheels (with permission, of course). Sit with the camera while your teammate pulls or pushes the chair. Hallways are very flat, perfect for smooth dolly shots. Watch those stairs!

Dolly 2 Dust off your little red wagon. Sit inside and hold the camera while someone *slowly* pulls the wagon. Use the flattest possible surface, like a paved driveway. For smoother shots, keep your elbows up; your arms will absorb some bumps. Make sure you don't fall off the wagon. Oil those squeaky wheels first!

How to Hold Your Camera

If your camera has an image stabilization feature, turn it on, unless you're faking an earthquake. As the name implies, this magic feature helps keep things steady even if you have hiccups. Use it.

Slow, smooth motions

Yo! This part is important. Don't make your audience seasick. You need to practice your camera moves until they are very smooth. Be sure the camera is steady and recording for at least two seconds before you move it in any direction. Then start moving the camera in a single smooth motion. Keep a constant slow speed as you *tilt* (camera up and down) or *pan* (camera side to side). Come to a smooth, slow stop before ending the shot. Always pause for two seconds before you stop the recording (you may need those extra seconds later for an editing effect or for setting up the next shot). It's wise to use a tripod (or one of the other "pods" described on pages 27–29). That's the easiest way to get pro-looking camera moves without the shakes. Pod that camera!

BE A POD PERSON

In case you haven't heard, keep that camera steady until you want it to move. Here are ways of not moving. Pick a position that's comfortable.

Tripod

Three legs is the steadiest way to shoot. Most tripods have a handle to help you smoothly tilt and pan the camera once it's attached. Loosen the knobs before moving the camera, and tighten the knobs to lock the camera in place for a still shot. Whenever you move the tripod to a new set-up, remove the camera first and move it separately. The little screw isn't that dependable, so don't bet your camera on it. When you set up, make sure all three legs are locked before re-attaching your camera; otherwise *Boom! Crash!* Hey! It's time to buy a new camera.

Monopod

A monopod's like a walking stick that attaches to the camera. It keeps the camera from moving up and down but not side to side. Adjust to height, lock the pod, spread your feet or kneel, and hold it steady.

Minipod

These tiny tripods can fit in your pocket. They don't cost a lot. Attach the camera and set it on a flat surface like a table. Or fold the legs together and use it as a handle.

Kneepod

We propose you get down on one knee for a steady shot. Put the camera or your elbow on your knee. Don't sneeze.

Wallpod

Lots of professionals go steady against walls and doorways. It keeps them stable.

Chairpod

Sit the wrong way and take aim. Drives teachers crazy and makes the shot steadier, too.

Floorpod

Get on the ground and lie still. If you don't fall asleep, the camera won't shake.

Friendpod

Some friends bend over backwards for you. Others will bend forwards. Lean on one for a semi-steady shot.

GOOD

HORIZON DOWN LOW

PERSON ON RIGHT

GOOD

HORIZON UP HIGH

PERSON ON LEFT

BAD

EVERYTHING IN THE CENTER

What You See is What They Get

Get framed

When you look through the viewfinder, you frame your shot before you start to shoot.

You don't always have to move the camera to get your frame right. Use your zoom to set up your shot. The W is *wide angle*, far back, and T is *telephoto*, zoomed in close. For best results, keep in the middle of this range, maybe a bit closer to wide angle. Whenever you zoom in for a telephoto shot, less light can get down the lens tunnel into the camera.

You're a composer

Illustrators, painters, photographers, and movie directors agree: Anything you put in the frame has an effect on your viewer. How you *compose* or arrange your frame will help tell your story. People up close look intense. People far away look lonely. Someone who enters from off-camera can add surprise. (So can a flying pie.) Experiment with these visual tools. Every time you watch a movie or TV, see how they do it. You can even call it homework.

Tic-tac-toe

There's a simple rule for composing called The Rule of Thirds. Imagine a tic-tac-toe board on your frame.

- People's eyes should be about level with the top line across.
- The horizon or landscape line should be along either the top or bottom line.
- Put actors and key props or buildings along either of the two vertical lines.
- The Dead Zone is not just a Stephen King story; it's also the middle box on your grid. It's called that because it's a boring place. Nobody, and nothing important, should stay there for long. Keep your movie edgy. Keep things along the edges.

The Camera Shot List

To the right is a camera *shot list*. It's a list of all the camera shots in the future hit movie *Night of the Nurse*. If you make a shot list like this, your shoot will go much easier because your crew will know what to expect. All the initials are explained below.

This shot list features most of the basic camera moves you can make. Look closely. No shot is random. Each camera angle works to help tell its part of the story. And since the shots are helping tell the story, there's no need for much dialog.

Calling the shots

Use these initials on your own shot list. You'll learn them quickly. It'll take more time to learn how each of these shots can help make your story more powerful for your viewers. But it's really worth the time.

NIGHT OF THE NURSE

(ES) A building at night. The lights are on in the building.
(LS) The front door opens – our hero, a nurse, walks out and turns. She suddenly stops.
(MS) A sound! She reaches into her purse for something.
(CU) Her face shows fear as she looks around. We hear footsteps come closer.
(LS) Cut to the street-light shadow of a person walking slowly.
(P) The camera pans to the right, following the shadow until we reach its source: the legs and waist of a police officer.
(CU) A sigh of relief comes over our hero. She smiles.
(T) Tilt up from the legs to the officer's face. It's not the police. It's a uniformed werewolf!
(CA) Our hero's hands pulling a dog whistle from her purse.
(CU) She puts the whistle to her mouth.
(MS) Officer Werewolf covers his ears in pain.
(LS) The werewolf falls to the ground under the street light.
(CU) We see our hero's face as she screams, "No! No!"
(ZO) Zoom back from her face to see she's kneeling by the body – the dead werewolf is now a human policeman on the ground. She obviously loved him.
(TS) A different angle of our hero kneeling over the body. The camera holds a moment, then tracks further and further back, and they get smaller and smaller.
(FO) Fade to black.

(ES) Establishing shot

Also called a *wide shot*, it's used to start a new scene. It "establishes" where the action is taking place (a city, a lake, a building, a field). Think of all the movies that begin with a city skyline or a faraway shot of the school where the action will take place.

Establishing shot

Long shot

Medium shot

Close-up

(LS) Long shot

Show your talent from head to toe. Give us a look at the subjects from a slight distance without feeling too close to them. Good for introductions to characters and how they act in their world.

(MS) Medium shot

This is one of the most common shots, showing your talent from head to waist, like on a talk show. You can show one or two actors, or do an over-the-shoulder shot showing one side of a conversation.

(CU) Close-up

Head and shoulders, or even closer. This helps viewers really connect with the character, feeling his emotions. A lot of dialog is shot with "in your face" close-ups. Try an extreme close-up (ECU) showing just the eyes, which adds tension.

(P) Pan

When you pan, the camera pivots horizontally on the tripod, to the left or right. This gives viewers the feeling of looking for something and then finding it. Keep the camera motion slooooow and smooth.

(T) Tilt

To tilt, the camera pivots vertically on the tripod, up or down, head to toe or toe to head. Again, move as smoothly as possible.

(CA) Cutaway

Cutaway shots cut from the action to a detail and back, to reveal information to your viewers. They tell the story by hiding information and then revealing it in little bits. Say you see a sleeping dog. Cut away to a torn-up, empty box of dog biscuits on a table. Cut back to the sleeping dog and you get the big picture.

(TS) Tracking shot

In the tracking shot, you and the camera are traveling together. Walking's Okay, but a dolly (wheels) will be smoother. See page 26 for how to do it.

(FI) Fade-in
(FO) Fade-out

A fade-in (FI) occurs when the image slowly goes from black to light at the beginning of a scene, and a fade-out (FO) goes from light to black at the end. Some cameras have all kinds of interesting effects like these. They're fun, but they almost never help tell the story. Better to do your experimenting during editing (see pages 53–56), where you can remove those effects that make people throw up.

Tilt

Zoom Out

(W) Wipe

We don't use a wipe in *Night of the Nurse* (see page 31), but you've seen them often. That's when the next scene pops out of the last scene in a burst of technology. Maybe the new scene drops in from the top like an elevator coming down. Or a spiral twists, changing the old scene to the new one. Or the old image splits and opens like an elevator door, and inside the elevator is the new scene. Lots of cameras and video editing software have lots of wipe effects. They're fun to try, but if you go crazy with them, so will your audience.

(ZO) Zoom Out

Or (ZI) Zoom In. This is probably the most abused trick among new video directors. Use it wisely. Use your zoom mainly for setting up your shot before you shoot, not while recording.

As an effect, directors use snap zooming mainly for shock. *Zoop!* A snake in the cereal bowl! Sometimes, slow zooming can tell the story: Start close on your subject (a girl reading a comic book) and then slowly zoom wide to let us see what's really happening in the big picture (she's playing outfield in a softball game and the ball is landing behind her). It's strange to watch a zoom because our eyes don't move like that naturally. Don't zoom too much or viewers will zoom away.

Let There Be Lighting

For video, there's nothing more important than light. Without light, you end up with something called "dark." Today's cameras do a great job in low light and bright light. A few cameras can even shoot at night. By learning a little how light works with video, you'll not only avoid mistakes, you'll shine!

Don't mix and match light

Different kinds of light glow in different colors (see "Baby, Fire My Light" on page 39). Your camera can adjust to the color of the light because it has an automatic white balance feature. That means it works to make white things look white, even if there's yellowy light on them. Then all the other colors shift, too.

The main rule here is: Don't mix different kinds of light in one scene. You'll drive your camera insane (a little), and it might be way too obvious to your viewers that the colors, light, and tone are changing from shot to shot. Keep it consistent.

Light sources

Built-in light

Some cameras have a small built-in light. It's good for basic home movies, but for your super-professional show it's better as a *fill light* than as your main *key light*. (See "Light like a pro" on page 38.)

Indoor lights

Any of the lights in your house can help your shoot. Bare bulbs are good key lights, and lampshades fill in nicely. See "Light like a pro" (page 38) and "Baby, Fire My Light" (page 39) for more indoor lighting ideas.

Work lights

Clip-on work lights are great because they are easy to point at your talent. They (the lights) live in garages, basements, workrooms, or hardware stores. They don't cost a lot, and they really make a difference. Get permission to borrow or buy some.

Hot shoe light

Some cameras have a "hot shoe" – the flat, square silver attachment on top that holds an extra light. This light should sit a few inches higher than the lens. Charge it up first.

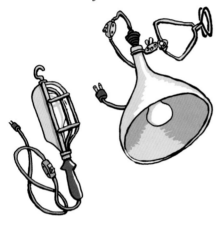

Night vision

Some cameras have an amazing infrared "night vision" feature that lets you shoot in near darkness. Everyone will look green, so we suggest using it in secret agent, military, or outer space scenes. Stand close to your subject for it to work well.

Daylight

The sun is great for light, but it's hard to move it where you need it. And the sun decides its own schedule. Good news: It's free and plentiful. Bad news: Sunlight puts deep shadows on people's faces. Cloudy skies or shade will help to soften shadows. See the "Reflect on This" tip on page 37 to erase shadows by using reflected sunlight. The pros try to shoot the whole of each scene on the same kind of day (sunny or cloudy) so it all looks the same when cut together.

Lighting problems/Lighting solutions

Problem: The mix of fluorescent and tungsten lights (see "Baby, Fire My Light" on page 39) makes your actors look half blue, half yellow, and all sick.

Solution: Turn off one type of light. Add more of the other type of light. The camera will be able to white-balance much better, bringing the actors back to health.

Problem: Direct sunlight is creating hard shadows on faces.

Solution: Have someone hold a reflector (see "Reflect on This," opposite) to shine sunlight from an angle that will brighten up the shadows.

Problem: The scary monster does not look scary enough.

Solution: You need darkness and weird shadows. A single light enhances shadows. Put a light near the floor for creepy face shadows. Light your subject from directly behind for a mysterious silhouette effect. Make the shot look dark by using very little lighting … maybe just a flashlight that sweeps around the shot, briefly shining on the sweaty kid in the monster mask.

Problem: It's too dark to shoot inside the room.

Solution: Change rooms. Or, borrow a clip light from the workshop, clip it to the seat of a chair, and keep it aimed where you need it. Remove the shade on a table lamp to make it a better light source. (Don't burn your fingers.) Open or shut curtains to control sunlight as needed. Try using your reflector inside, to help bounce sunlight or house lights onto your subject.

Blooper: Flare out!

If a bright light (especially the sun) shines into the camera lens, you'll get a big ugly streak in your picture called a lens flare. Keep your camera and light sources separated. If your talent stands in front of a light source, blocking it from shining into the lens (makes a cool silhouette effect), beware when she steps away – major lens flare!

Blooper: Sunstroke

Never point cameras at suns. It's bad for eyes, cameras, and viewers, in that order. Don't stare at the sun reflector either, even if you did build it.

Reflect on This – You can control the sun! (Sort of.) Make a homemade reflector by gluing or taping aluminum foil to one side of a big piece of cardboard. Have the dull side of the foil face out. It's actually better if the foil gets wrinkled, since you want to reflect diffused (spread-out) light rather than a direct blast of sun. Have the gaffer stand next to the camera and aim the reflector's light on an actor's face, until shadows get weaker. A silver sun shield from a car can make a good improvised light reflector, too.

Sunlight Delight – The sun can be either your back-light or key light. The reflector can provide your key light or fill light. Experiment to see what looks good in the camera. You may have to remind your gaffer to stand still during the takes so you don't end up with a disco ball effect. Two reflectors can be better than one in some cases. If you only have one gaffer, try leaning the other reflector against a wall or tree.

No light

Light like a pro

Your best bet is to use existing light. (Translation: Shoot your video where there is already a bunch of light.) But if you want to learn lighting, here's the Hollywood way.

It's called *three-point lighting*: three lights in three different places aimed at the middle, and *presto!* they mostly erase each other's shadows. Hard shadows are bad stuff in videos, except in monster and bad-guy stories.

The three lights of this system are:

Key light – The first and brightest light, usually pointing at the subject. A work light, or a 100-watt bulb without a shade, would make a good key light.

Fill light – The second light, half as bright, is placed opposite the key light on the other side of the camera. It softens most of the shadows cast by the key light. A basic work light with a 50-watt bulb, or a lamp with a shade, can do the trick.

Backlight – The third light is set behind the talent, to help them stand out from the background. Don't shine it directly into the camera lens. A lamp (with a shade) in the background would make a good backlight for you. You can even keep it visible in the frame.

If you can't get all three lights set up, try just a key and a fill light. No? Just a key light, then. No? Use the light on your camera. Or the sun. Or the refrigerator light …

Key light

Key light + fill light

Key light + fill light + backlight

38

BABY, FIRE MY LIGHT

It's a little advanced, but it's good to know some basic types of light, and their effect on your video. Try not to mix them in a shot. Here they are, starting with the good and ending with the not so good.

LIGHT: Daylight
WHAT IT IS: A brilliant golden light from our local star.
GOOD FOR: Exterior daytime shooting, day-for-night shooting (see "Nighttime in daytime" on page 46), shooting inside rooms with lots of windows.

LIGHT: LED
WHAT IT IS: A blue-white light from Light Emitting Diodes.
GOOD FOR: All purposes. Many cameras now have built-in LED lights. They provide lots of light for very little energy, so batteries won't die quite so quickly.

LIGHT: Halogen
WHAT IT IS: A brilliant white light bulb found in many desk and floor lamps.
GOOD FOR: Everything … Halogen mixes pretty well with daylight, too. It's the lamp most frequently used by pros.

LIGHT: Tungsten
WHAT IT IS: The normal everyday light bulb. These regular light bulbs have a warm, yellowish light.
GOOD FOR: Shooting indoors when that's what's available. Looks "homey."

LIGHT: Fluorescent
WHAT IT IS: A blue-white light from tube bulbs.
GOOD FOR: Shooting inside schools, stores, or bathrooms, where we expect that kind of light. Usually makes people look pale or cold. Good for sick characters.

LIGHT: Neon
WHAT IT IS: Tubes filled with gas. Can be shaped to say *Open All Night* or *Drive-up Window* in cool colors.
GOOD FOR: Gritty urban drama, with wailing saxophones and tough kids wearing sunglasses all night long.

Remember, consistent light is better than perfect light.

TEST 1, 2, 3...

Sound Recording

Good sound is just as important as good lighting. It's frustrating to not understand the actors, and distracting noises always distract. But if you do it right, you'll hear applause from your audience.

Sound advice

- Quiet on the set!
- No heavy breathing behind the camera. No eating, either. Stop it right now.
- Get the mic as close to your talent as possible.
- Listen on headphones while you're shooting (if the camera has a headphone jack).
- Was that a jet overhead? Play back your takes to make sure the sound was recorded well. The time to shoot another take is before moving on to shoot the next scene.

Built-in microphones

All cameras have built-in microphones, often a little pinhole near the front of your camera. This type of mic will pick up every sound from every direction, so don't mutter insults at the actors. For general shooting, the built-in mic is good enough ... and one less thing to worry about. Some new shooters stick their fingers on or around the mic. This will sound *awful*! Hands off.

Blooper: Call me mic

You thought it should be spelled "mike," right? Well, you're a pro now, so it's "mic." But it sounds like "mike."

External microphones

If your camera has a mic input jack, then think about taking your sound to the next level. An external microphone makes a big difference because it brings the voice and the mic into close range. It can be a hand-held mic for interviews, or a little mic that hides on someone's shirt or a nearby prop.

You can spend a week's allowance – or a year's, depending on your allowance. Even an inexpensive mic will be a sound investment. (Get one at your local electronics megabox.)

In addition to your mic, get an extension cord of at least 10 meters (30 feet). Then you can set up your shot and have enough cord to snake back to the camera. If you don't want your mic and all that cord to be seen by the camera, your best bet is a boom (see "Make a Sonic Boom," on page 42). You might be able to borrow a wireless mic from school or the opera. There's no cord to trip over, but you'll need a lesson in using one, along with some spare batteries.

How to Fake a Wireless Mic

In Hollywood movies, the sound is often recorded separately and added to the video during editing. Believe it or not, you can use this double system without a special mic. This is handy if your camera mic is too far from your actors. Once the mic is more than an arm's length away, your audio quality will start to decline.

■ Your audio recorder can be a small voice memo recorder, or a mobile phone with a voice memo feature.

■ Put the recorder on or near the actors. Make sure it's recording during your take. If you can connect an actual mic, even better.

■ Shoot: Have one of the actors in the shot clap hands and say the shot and take number. You'll need this to sync the sound during editing.

■ Check: After the take, listen to the sound on the audio recorder to make sure it's clear. If not, position the audio recorder's mic closer to the actors for the next take.

■ Edit: Bring the matching audio and video files of each take into the timeline of your editing software. Use the fine controls to match the sound of the clap in the audio to the video. Once the matching audio tracks are in sync with each other, turn off the poorer sound that came from the video camera.

Voilà, you have a double-system shot, just like the pros.

Did you know?

Back in the 1920s, the cameras for the first sound films made too much noise. Camera operators had to put their clackety-clacking cameras in a booth behind glass so everything wouldn't sound like a machine gun.

IF YOU CLAP FIRST, WE SYNC. IF YOU DON'T, WE SINK.

Make a Sonic Boom

How to keep a good mic near the action but out of sight? Build a boom mic. Connect a good microphone to a broomstick with all that duct tape you've got. Make sure your cable's long enough. A 10-meter (30-foot) audio extension should be plenty. If you have a telescoping aluminum painting pole, that's even better than a broomstick. Have someone hold the whole thing out of view, above the actors' heads, off camera. It takes strong arms and good ears. After each take, play it back to check how the sound sounded.

Testing, 1, 2, 3

Before you begin shooting, take a test. See how your audio microphone can handle any task you've got for it. Keep everything on your audio checklist ready, so no one's kept waiting.

Audio checklist

- Headphones
- Headphone extension cord if the audio person is not also operating the camera
- External mic (and any plug adapters you need)
- External mic extension cord
- Boom pole (if you're using one; see "Make a Sonic Boom," opposite)
- Extra batteries for battery-powered mics
- Audio-To-Go wagon or travel case

Blooper: Crash and flush

Don't walk too far when headphones or microphones are wired to the camera. *Crash!* Lots of otherwise smart people forget, and wreck their equipment. Also, if you're using a wireless mic, make sure your talent turns it off before taking a bathroom break. Or don't, and save the waterfall for your bloopers reel.

MAKE A MUSIC VIDEO!

Most music videos are done like karaoke. The song is recorded first. The singers don't have to sing in the video; they just need to move their lips and try to act as convincing as possible. Here are some quick tips for making your own very valuable videos.

■ Start with a pre-recorded song. If it's not your own creation, use one from a favorite artist or band.

■ Play the song out loud for the "singers." Play it often enough so everyone knows how their lips are supposed to be singing/syncing.

■ Work out your theme. What's it going to be? Seventies disco clothes? Nineties grunge? Vampires? Zombies? Disco zombies?

■ Come up with a story. Not a big story, but something that has a beginning (for instance: someone arrives), a middle (there's a problem), and an end (the problem is solved). Decide who is playing what part, if you're going that way.

■ Storyboard the key shots. Figure out the interesting angles. See what else pops into your mind. In most videos, a single shot is usually no longer than five seconds.

■ Shoot the band, or your actors pretending to play the song like a band, or act out the parts of the story. Also, capture your actors doing other interesting or goofy stuff that you might not know what to do with. Video anything else you think would be fun or useful, even clouds and trees and cars going by. You can use some of it later for filling in spaces during the edit.

■ In editing, start with the exact same recording of the song. Sync each video segment with the song, then go into the settings for that segment and turn off its audio. Try your best to match the lips to the lyrics.

■ Mix and match the best segments until the entire soundtrack is covered with video.

■ Play it back and win every contest you ever enter. Unless the original musicians ask you to take it off the Internet. Then ya gotta.

A stampede of 200 wild horses charging through downtown. A huge ship made from trees by beavers. An intergalactic car wash. Someday you may have the chance to direct these special effects in a movie. Until then, let's see what you can do without blowing your allowance.

Some great special effects can be created while you are shooting. No computers, no animation, and no fortune required.

Live Visual Effects

No one expects your movie to look as good as a Hollywood feature, but with a little cleverness you will keep your audience (and your team) psyched. Here are a few visual tricks that are also treats:

- Shoot your action in a reflective surface like a car window, a mirror, a swimming pool, or other water. Then pull back to show the "real" world and continue the action.
- Put your camera on its side. Then pretend the floor is a wall and the wall is a floor. Whoops, did you drop something?
- Pretend the camera is a person. Have your actors talk to it, looking straight into the lens. Have the camera operator (or an off-screen actor) say the "camera's" lines. Let the camera take a walk. Just keep it at eye level, and don't trip over anything.
- Pretend the camera is a dog and the viewer sees everything through its eyes. Get down on the ground and wander. Watch that fire hydrant!
- Take a flexible mirror made of aluminum foil or a sheet of reflective Mylar. Hold it at a 45° angle in front of the camera lens with your subject at a 90° angle from the camera. Zoom all the way in, so that all you can see is the reflection in the mirror. Bend the mirror to achieve wavy, distorted images while shooting. Great for segments showing your character dreaming or being crazy.

Know all the angles

These effects don't take any effort at all. And they'll give you more ways to tell your story.

- Put the camera near the ground and point up. Low angles make things look taller, and make bad guys look badder.
- Put the camera up high and point down. Make a character seem weak, small, or in danger. Make a toy building look real (depending on the toy).
- Show your characters against the sky, with no other background. They'll look like they're on a mountaintop.
- Show a character. Cut away (see the example opposite) to a beehive, or a python, or a cafeteria lady. Now cut back to the character, who looks scared, right? Your viewers add up the different pieces for extra impact. Now replace that python with a birthday cake. The footage of the actor is identical, but you'll swear the character is thinking about blowing out candles this time.

SHOT 1

THIS SHOT 2 **OR** THAT SHOT 2

SHOT 3

From weather to weapons

Need that perfect effect to get your story across? Here are a few favorites:

Snow job

Does your movie need a snowfall? Try instant mashed potato flakes. Frame a close-up of your hero, and have a crew member sprinkle the potato flakes just above the shot, near the lens. Is it a blizzard? An electric fan on an off-screen table makes an instant blizzard! Substitute dry leaves for the potato flakes if it's fall. Change the wind by moving your fan closer or farther away. Watch those fingers!

To show snow on the ground, don't waste all those potato flakes. Shoot winter scenes in the winter and summer scenes in the summer. *Work with what you've got* is the key to happiness and staying sane in moviemaking.

Earthquake

Put lots of things on a table. Have a few people crouch down and shake the legs while the camera operator shakes the camera *very slightly*. The actors should stumble around as if they feel the floor under them quaking. This is how they shot the battle scenes in many classic science fiction shows. It's low budget and it really works.

Wind, hurricane, tornado, breeze

Use a fan. Don't cut off your fingers. Period.

Rain

Set a garden hose to the rain setting. Spray it in front of the camera or filter it slowly through a colander held above the frame. *Keep the camera covered and dry or you'll be wringing out your piggy bank.*

After the rain

Driveways and sidewalks look slick and dramatic when they're wet. The wet surfaces catch the light for great effect. (The lone hero always makes his final exit on a wet street.) Use a garden hose to wet the driveway or sidewalk – NOT the kitchen – and don't give control of the water to the wrong kid or you'll be hosed!

Nighttime in daytime

Need night but need to see? Use the manual exposure control to make your picture look dark, or add a night-time effect during editing. In the camera settings, or on the computer, you can adjust the color or white balance to make the picture look blue. How? RTM. To make it look more convincing, shoot on a cloudy day or just after sunset to avoid hard shadows. This technique is called day-for-night shooting.

Gone and back

How do you make someone (or something) vanish? Put the camera on a tripod or completely steady surface and record your scene. At the director's hand signal (no noise, please) all action freezes and the camera operator stops recording. The actor (or thing) disappears and recording begins again. You can also add people in the scene in the same way. This will take a little practice.

Attack props

For some reason, modern filmmakers need to make movies about characters whacking each other with solid objects. If you must go after each other with weapons, make them out of Styrofoam and color them. (When you buy a TV or computer or microwave, there's lots of good Styrofoam.) Or get inflatables. DON'T use actual hard objects, okay?

Stunts

Car chases! Kung fu moves! Jumping through a glass window! Picking up a piano and throwing it – while someone is playing it! Want to do these stunts? Here's all you have to do: Drink a nice warm cup of milk, have a nap, and *dream* about them. Did you think the authors were going to tell you how to do anything even remotely like that? Stick with the Styrofoam.

MASHED POTATO FLAKES

WEATHER: RAIN NOW, SNOW LATER

LAWYERS' NOTE: The authors really wanted to tell you how to do stunts. This made the lawyers laugh very hard. AUTHORS' NOTE: Camera angles, montage, and clever editing can make lame, lawyer-approved stunts look better than you'd expect. Practice, practice, practice.

Sound Effects

Since the glory days of radio, great sound effects have been an art form. Make it real. Make it fun. Just don't let your sound effects drown out the dialog.

Here are a few effects to experiment with:

Wind: Exhale gently through your teeth near the mic.

Explosion/Thunder: Vibrate the back of your tongue and exhale/gargle on the mic not so gently. Every kid knows how to make this noise, but it's impossible to describe.

Fire: Keep crunching and releasing a ball of plastic wrap near the mic.

Rain: Put dried beans in a tambourine drumhead and roll them slowly above the mic. First tape down the jingles so they don't jangle.

Telephone voice: Cup your hands or speak into a cup near the microphone. Let your nose vibrate as you talk. Or, put a mic against a phone and call yourself.

Background sounds: Use a dedicated voice recorder or a cell phone with a voice memo feature (add a mic, if you like) to record the real world: nature sounds, machines, traffic, classroom sounds, lunchroom chattering, etc. Your actors could be parked in the driveway and it'll sound like they're in a car chase. Add the sounds at editing time (see pages 50–61).

Pro noise: Borrow a sound effects CD from your local library. There are plenty to choose from, even special ones for Halloween. Or download sound effects files off the web. From doors creaking to mice squeaking to balloons leaking, it's all waiting for you.

For the best control of your sound effects, collect or record them individually and edit them into your video after you're done shooting (see page 55).

Direct Challenge

So you're the director. Yes, the director calls the shots. That doesn't make you the big shot, but it's big work. Treat people well or you'll be directing traffic instead. Remember, you're not an emperor – you're just the kid with the video camera. So what's in store for you?

- Directing is a fun challenge. You get to see your ideas come to life. And you get to tell stories that are important to you.
- It takes planning, planning, planning. Nobody wants to sit around while you make up your mind – or make up the next idea. Get it all ready before you get going.
- Delegate. Which means, divvy up the jobs.
- Focus, good communication, hard work – sounds like Scouting, and in a way it is. Be prepared, and be open to other people's suggestions or they won't play.
- The director decides what stays and what goes, and should do it in a fair and smart way. Your decisions should be in the best interest of the story and of the people working with you. Not because it's your camera. Ya know?

Directing Checklist

- Plan ahead. Write things down and make copies for your team. It *really* helps.
- Provide clear directions to your team during the shoot.
- Divvy up the jobs fairly and effectively.
- Be considerate of the time and patience of your team.
- Feed your team if it's your show. Hungry volunteers quit quickly.
- Have backup plans if you get stuck.
- Don't hog all the credit. It's a team effort!

Calling the Shots – The Director's Lines

Like the actors, the director has lines to say on the set. Get them right!

- ◾ "**Ready on the set**" – Let the team know you're ready to take a shot. Everyone should take their positions and be quiet and alert.
- ◾ "**Roll camera**" – Tells the camera operator (if it's not you) to start recording. She responds by saying "Rolling."
- ◾ "**Action**" – Tells the actors to start performing.
- ◾ "**Cut**" – Says the shot is over. The camera operator stops recording and everyone prepares for what's next.
- ◾ "**It's a wrap**" – Means the shooting session is over, or maybe, "Hey, everyone, burritos for lunch!"

Viewing the "Dailies"

Did you get what you need? If not, when else will you shoot it? During the shoot (or maybe after shooting each scene), set the camera to playback mode and take a close look at what you shot. If you didn't get what you need, shoot another take. Use the headphones to be sure it sounds all right.

WHEN IT ALL GOES WRONG, USE THE WRONG NAME

Unfortunately, Hollywood is full of directors who haven't read *Attack of the Killer Video Book* … yet. So naturally, their movies sometimes end up a mess. For years, dozens of directors have used the official, approved "I withdraw my name" name: Alan Smithee. Search his name online for a laugh. If your movie comes out less than desired, now you know whose name to put on it. Since he's not real, he'll never sue you.

SUCCESSFUL DIRECTORS MIND THEIR P's AND Q's:

Patience (it takes time)
Persistence (it takes work)
Permission (it takes the heat off)
Pleasantness (a dumb word, but we're stuck with P's here. You don't want a crew mutiny.)
Quirkiness (it takes humor to make humor)
Quality (make it a movie to be proud of)
Quickness (don't be so nuts about quality that you drive people nuts)

Remember to keep things fun for all the people who are helping to bring your moviemaking vision to life.

IT'S PLAYBACK TIME!

POST-PRODUCTION

Post Overview

Post means *after*. As in, *after your production*. In Hollywood, post-production (usually called *post*) includes everything you do to polish an epic movie. POST is:

- **Transferring** (downloading) your shots from your camera into your computer.
- **Collecting** a video and audio library of all your source material for the edit session.
- **Editing** with video editing software.
- **Reshooting** missing segments or special effects such as green-screen segments (see page 58).
- **Creating** optional finishing touches such as titles, captions, sound effects, and any special effects.
- **Sharing** your finished video by uploading online or having a show.
- **Publicizing** your video and entering kid video festivals.

It almost always takes less time to shoot a movie than to edit it in post-production, if you want the end result to look good.

Transfer

Once you've shot all your video (or the storage on your camera is full), you'll need to download the files to a computer. This may happen several times during your shoot.

There are many ways to transfer your video files from your camera to your computer. Always RTM.

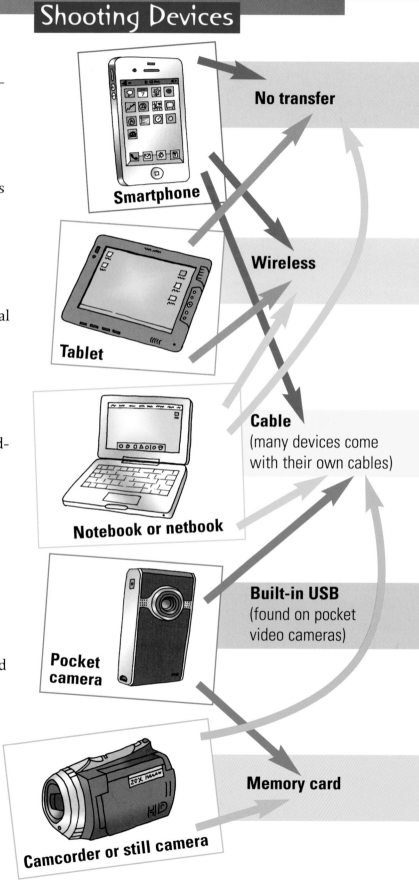

Smartphone

No transfer

Wireless

Tablet

Notebook or netbook

Cable
(many devices come with their own cables)

Pocket camera

Built-in USB
(found on pocket video cameras)

Memory card

Camcorder or still camera

TRANSFER MATRIX

How To

Pros and Cons

Editing Devices

If you recorded video right to a device where you're also going to be doing the editing, then there's no transfer to be done!

Saves download time. The editing will probably take a lot longer on an underpowered mobile device than on a powerful notebook or desktop computer.

Smartphone

Turn on your wireless capability (Bluetooth or Wi-Fi) on both your camera and computer. Use your media software to download the files, or copy over by hand. Unmount the device from your desktop to safely eject it. Erase or format the memory in the camera.

No cable or card to misplace. Operating your microwave oven or other RF-emitting devices at the same time can interfere with the transfer. But you'll have hot chocolate for everyone!

Tablet

Plug the USB cable into the camera and the computer. Turn on the camera. Use your media management software to download the files, or copy them over by hand. Unmount the camera from your desktop to safely eject it. Erase or format the memory in the camera.

If you lose the cable, you're in *biiiiig* trouble. This may be a slower way to download large files as opposed to moving the camera's card.

Notebook or netbook

Pop the little USB jack out of the side of your camera. Plug it into your computer's USB port. Use your media management software to download the files, or copy them over by hand. Unmount the card from your desktop to safely eject it. Erase or format the memory in the camera.

There's no cable or removable card to lose. If your built-in RAM or memory card gets full during your shoot, everyone will need to take a break while the camera rests. Once you download the files and wipe the memory, you can start again.

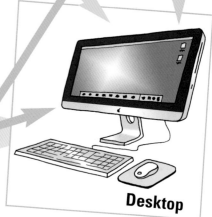

Desktop

Turn off your camera. Remove the card and put it into a card reader slot connected to your computer. Use your media management software to download the files, or copy over by hand. Safely eject the card and return it to the camera. Erase or format the card in the camera.

This is one of the fastest ways to transfer files from a camera to a computer. Finding an external card reader can sometimes be a challenge.

Tips when downloading and managing your files

- On some computers, an app will launch automatically to manage importing your files.
- If you don't have this app (or don't want to use it), copy the files manually by dragging them from the camera media to the proper folder on your hard drive.
- Organize your files. Adding keywords helps you search through a growing video library. Add a keyword ("blah" or "yuck") for shots you probably won't use. Add keywords like "supremo" or "awesome-tacular" for your favorite takes. Got a storyboard with shot numbers? Add the correct shot numbers to each shot. (FYI, "R2-D2" was the sound editor's keywords – meaning "Reel 2, Dialog 2" – which George Lucas kept hearing during an edit.)
- Fortunately, each clip will have icons of a single frame to help you find shots without keywords. In Hollywood, the clapperboard is the first thing you see, so you know which clip you've got.
- Once the files are safely in your computer, THEN you can delete the camera's memory files. To be extra safe, you might want to make backups of all files on an external hard drive.

Editing

The shooting's over and you're the last one standing. You've got all the footage. It's a movie now, right? Maybe, and maybe not.

Editing is where a lot of movie magic takes place. *Editing* means selecting the best takes and putting them all together (with sound, music, and any effects) to create a finished show. We suggest you begin your editing early on, after your first shooting session. By starting your editing early in the process, you'll learn about what to do better before your actors have to go home for dinner.

It may seem like putting together a puzzle the first time you edit a film. It takes experience (and software) to edit like the pros. Bad editing can often ruin a bunch of good shots. Good editing can *sometimes* save a bunch of bad shots.

EDITING IS THE LAST REWRITE

EDIT to keep the story moving.

EDIT out all the unnecessary moments.

EDIT to focus on the drama, the humor, the story you're telling.

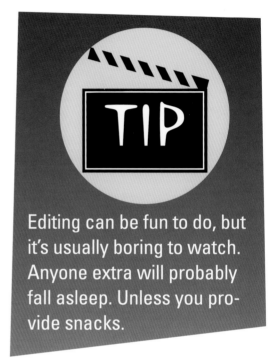

Editing can be fun to do, but it's usually boring to watch. Anyone extra will probably fall asleep. Unless you provide snacks.

First shot (MS)

Second shot (LS)

Third shot (CU)

Video Editing Software

There are tons of digital video editing software apps. You want nonlinear editing (NLE) tools, because linear editing (LE) is for tape and film, okay? (T&F, OK?)

Search Wikipedia for "video editing software." You'll find an up-to-date list of the most common editing apps. On a tight budget? There are links to free downloads. Fortunately, these apps share many common concepts and terms – what you learn from one, you can use somewhere else.

The fact is, technology changes all the time. The following steps are valid today but will probably become outdated by Thursday. If any terms here seem like gibberish, sorry. Check the glossary or go online. There's no time to explain – it's a short book. Also, some of these terms are brand names. We aren't endorsing any specific brands, sadly.*

Actually, we tried to get a software company to sponsor a "mention," but they wouldn't give us their money. Or their software. Or a return phone call.

Basic Stages of Editing

Collect your libraries

Depending on your editing app, this may be automatic, or you may need to "add to library" or "import" for each new batch of clips. You should have a video library and an audio library set up.

Arrange in the timeline

The *timeline* is the editor's best friend. It's a visual layout of all your video clips in the order you want. Think of each video clip as a bead; the timeline strings the necklace together. To use it, drag each clip from your library into your timeline.

Trim your clips

Don't want the entire shot? Once you clip it, it's called a *clip*. You can set the start and end points that you want, using the *clip trimmer controls* or *precision editor*. Now what you have is the *range* of your clip.

Cut or transition?

Cuts are changes in camera set-up in a scene where time and space remain the same. *Transitions* are mainly used to show how time (or location) has changed.

Cuts should be invisible, without tricky effects. That's called a *hard cut*. Transitions are distracting and should generally be avoided (you can simply cut from one scene to the next), but they're so much fun it's hard not to use them. Lots of transitions (wipes, fades, dissolves, etc.) are easily found in your *transitions library*, represented by icons.

The most common and least objectionable transition is called a *dissolve*. In the timeline, double-click a transition to change its settings.

Watch any professional video: movies, TV, music, even commercials, and see for yourself the difference between cuts and transitions.

Effects are special

Double-click a clip in the timeline to adjust its audio and video. You can also apply various filters to make your video look scratchy like old film, romantically soft and fuzzy, or dreamlike. You can even change the color, turn it upside down, and tons of other hideous choices.

Zounds! Add sounds

Drag a piece of music or a sound effect from your audio library to the timeline. Double-click it to adjust the audio levels. Want to make sure the music won't overpower the dialog? Some video editing apps have a feature called *ducking*, which sets the music volume automatically. Hey, music! Duck!

TIP

Don't use too many fancy transitions. Most clips don't need transitions between them.

When you cut between two shots of the same subject from slightly different camera angles, it's called a *jump cut*. It can look like a mistake, but arty directors like to use the technique to create a deliberately jarring effect.

The Incredible Killer Sweater from Outer Space - Script - page 3

3 takes - use second (tape counter 5:33)

SHOT 08: MS
INT. KITCHEN - BERNIE'S HOUSE - SAME TIME
A sweater flies through the air and lands on a chair with an om... WHOOSH! As it settles, we hear footsteps approaching.
EFFECTS: ominous WHOOSH, footsteps

4 takes - use last one (starts at 10:26)

SHOT 09: LS
Bernie enters the kitchen.
BERNIE: (to himself) Now how did this sweater get over here?
Bernie picks up the sweater and pulls it on over his head as scary music builds.
SOUND EFFECT: scary music

only one take - use it! (16:22)

SHOT 10: CU
The alien sweater monster tightens at the neck! Bernie struggles and clutches and grunts, then falls to the floor.
BERNIE: Umph! Ugh! Argh! Oomf!

Preview and fine-tune

See your movie in progress – just hit the *play* button. You'll preview things to fine-tune and adjust. So adjust them, then hit *play* again, Sam. And again. "Tweak and twack" are not Muppets, but they are video vocabulary words you should look up. Now. Then tweak and twack until it's twonderful.

Export options, rendering, and uploading

Sometimes called *finalize project*, rendering is the final step, the glue to all your tweaks, twacks, changes, and effects. When you render, you make the new, finished video file. It may take an hour, or several. Do this before heading to sleep or when you don't need to use the computer for other things.

8½ steps to editing success
Here's a summary of the key points of editing:

1. Shoot enough extra coverage (also called "more than enough video") so you get what you need (see page 26). You won't always know what you've got until you're in the editing stage. Practice.

2. After each take, watch the previous shot to make sure you got it right. If it's not good enough, shoot it again.

3. Download and collect all the video files into your video software editing library. (See the Transfer Matrix on page 51.)

4. Drag the shots – in order – into your timeline.

5. Trim the beginning and ending of each shot and keep previewing until the action flows well and feels right.

6. Add simple transitions between scenes, as well as a fade-in from black at the beginning, and a fade-out to black at the end.

7. Add a soundtrack of music and sound effects to help your story. Don't mix the music so loud you can't hear the dialog.

8. Get feedback. Listen to suggestions and edit again. Render the finished movie. Happy? Schedule a premiere or upload it to the Internet.

8½. Carry an autograph pen to the premiere and start wearing sunglasses indoors.

MAKE A MOVIE TRAILER

A trailer isn't just a comfy RV for movie stars on the set. It's also an ad for the movie that usually runs a minute or two. Some popular editing apps (such as iMovie) have a template that will help you quickly edit an almost-professional movie trailer. Here's how it works.

- There are different styles of trailer templates. Preview them and pick one.
- Use *storyboard* or *shot list* views. Drag a shot from your video library onto each of the storyboard frames.
- Hit *play* or *preview* to see the movie trailer in progress.
- Replace so-so clips with better ones, or change the start times of a clip so it will fit better.
- Keep previewing and tweaking until you're happy with your trailer.
- Open the project in *outline* view, and enter all the names for your movie titles, movie studio, cast members, director, and crew. Don't forget to thank Mark and Hazlitt.
- Finalize your project and render your finished trailer. This process may take an hour or all night, depending on how high your resolution is.
- Upload the rendered trailer to a video-sharing site to let the whole world, and Mom, see your work (see pages 62–63 for more on Sharing).

TIP

This is the quickest way to make a polished one-minute clip with professional titles, music, and editing. You can learn a lot by studying how these templates put a movie together. You may like your trailer so much, you'll want to make the whole movie next.

Did you know?

They're called *trailers* because, before the 1960s, movie promo ads ran at the end of the feature movie, not before. What ran before the movie — cartoons, newsreels, short Three Stooges films — were called *leaders*. Ask your grandparents.

You can use a bedsheet only if it matches this bright green.

Green Screen

You know how movie superheroes fly, right? They stand in front of a green screen (also called chroma-key), and then the movie of the city is put behind them later, by computer. The computer "ignores" the green screen and replaces it with whatever image you add. And you can add it, too. Here's how:

Pre-production

- Buy a piece of special green-screen fabric from a photography or fabric store. Or, if you have a flat wall and permission to paint it, buy green-screen paint.
- While you're out getting permission, ask if it's cool to put pinholes in the wall. Hang the fabric, securing with push-pins around the edges and making sure there are no wrinkles or visible seams. Smoothly round the cloth where the wall meets the floor. If you can only get a small piece of fabric, set it up for shooting something miniature on a tabletop.
- Set up ambient lights so that the green surface is evenly lit without shadows (see page 38).

Production

- Point your camera at the green screen. It's best to use a tripod so the entire view on the camera's display is green.
- Record your talent (or miniature) sitting, standing, or acting between the green screen and the camera.

Post-production

- If you have access to green-screen features in your video editing software, turn them on. (In iMovie, go to Preferences and click the checkbox next to "Show Advanced Tools.")
- Drag your background image file (still or video) onto the timeline. For a still image, increase the duration to the same length as your green-screen action shot.
- Drag your green-screen action clip to the timeline so it's on top of your background.
- Click *play* to preview the overlay.
- If needed, use the video adjustments on the green-screen clip to improve the effect.

A tiny green screen

If you can't find a screen, you can still find the green!

■ Fill your computer's screen with a solid bright green color and adjust the screen brightness as necessary. One way is to use PDF software or a word processor (really!) and set the background to match our solid green sample. Or google "Chromakey" for samples. Choose Full Screen Mode. Zoom in to fill the entire screen with green.

■ Hold your camera in one hand so that only green is visible through the display. Hit record and speak in a funny voice while acting with your sock puppet, or action figure, between the screen and the camera.

■ Using a tripod will make it possible to have a conversation with two characters, one on each hand.

■ Import your clip into your editing program and drop an exotic or unpredictable background into the green screen.

Post Effects and CGI

Will motion graphics or CGI animate you?

The benefit: Animations don't need any (or many) actors, you get more control of your video's look, and your imagination is the limit.

The truth: You'll invest a lot of time learning your software, not just camcording, and spend plenty more time actually completing your video.

Motion graphics usually means 2D animation, and CGI means computer-generated imagery – usually 3D animation.

Search "motion graphics" and "3D computer graphics software" on Wikipedia for lists of software and animation tools. Some are free.

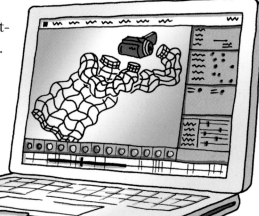

■ **Motion graphics steps:** You'll usually need flat artwork and typography made in apps like Illustrator or Flash, or an image editor like Photoshop. Most fancy movie title sequences are done by teams of motion graphics artists.

■ **CGI steps** could include 3D modeling, texture mapping, virtual lighting, animation, and rendering. Most 3D animated cartoons are made by different teams of CGI artists with big budgets. It's a whole world a whole lot bigger than this book. Explore it!

Post-production: Sound

You (or your friend with the audio software) can "sweeten" and mix your soundtrack. *Sweeten* means "make it sound better." Sweet.

Sound level too low or too high on your original footage? No problem. Using editing software, you can adjust levels to bring up the volume on the too-quiet spots and at the same time use *compression* to bring the too-loud spots down to bearable levels. You can sometimes nip this problem in the bud by using your camera's *limiter* or *auto-gain* features to help you keep the audio levels under control while you are shooting.

Other things you can experiment with during audio post-production:

■ Add original or borrowed music.
■ Add original sound effects, or get them online or from library CDs.
■ Record and add narration.
■ Replace bad dialog mistakes.
■ Remove sounds you accidentally recorded during the shoot (like car horns, your laughing crew, or words that will get you in trouble).

Blooper: Shoot! I have to reshoot?

To improve your movie, you may need to reshoot some shots. The good news: Practice makes perfect. You should be able to shoot much faster the second time around. It's more fun for your crew to work fast anyway, like sled dogs. Yell "Mush!" if they slow down.

For reshoots, think about continuity. Your actors need to have their clothes look the same, and hold the same props in the same way. If things don't match when you edit them together, and the actor's drink seems to keep refilling itself, that's called a continuity problem, or a "mess." Mistakes are always welcome on your bloopers reel.

Post-production: Titles

Titles feature the name of the video and the people who made it. Titles often appear at the beginning (main titles) and end (end titles). They can be an art form in themselves, and a fun start for your video. Or you may want easy titles that just get the information across.

The name game

Rule #1 for short movies: Your titles should be shorter than your video. Keep most titles onscreen no longer than three seconds each, or a bit longer if there's lots written on them. Try to use as few as possible; however, a young video genius we know says, "Titles make the movie." Your call. Here are the key title cards to include:

- The movie's name (*A Bongo Family Thanksgiving*)
- The director (*Directed by Jojo Bongo*)
- The writer (*Written by Bobo Bongo*)
- The actors (*Starring Bobo, Mo, Flo & Dodo Bongo*)
- The crew's names and main jobs on the movie (*Camera Operator: Yoyo Bongo*)
- Legal notice (*Copyright ©2020 by Jojo Bongo. All rights reserved. Any resemblance to the real Bongo family is a totally freaky coincidence. Hear that, Dad?*)

Basics for editing in your titles

- Drag a title template into your timeline between two clips.
- Edit the text and add any new text you want to use.
- Add or tweak any text animation effects.
- Preview and tweak to perfection.
- The End.

Congratulations! You have earned your own killer space sweater. Wear it carefully.

THE BIG SHOW

Spreading the word

Your movie is "in the can." It is now ready for distribution. How do you get it out to the world?

- Go viral by uploading and sharing on social networking sites and media-sharing services.
- Stage a public screening for your class, friends, family, or even the unwashed public.
- Publicize your showing or online premiere with posters, e-mail campaigns, and event calendars.
- Send out a press release to your school paper, local newspapers and magazines, or kid-friendly news sites.

Post-production: sharing

- Uploading your finished productions to a video-sharing site is the quickest way to show your friends or the whole world what you've done.
- Create an account on YouTube or one of the many other sites that allow you to share your videos for free. Get adult permission first.
- When the upload is done, your video will be live. Choose a good time to upload. Think about when your friends and followers and loyal servants are online. Afternoons? After dinners? After midnights? Make sure it won't be buried under newer postings too soon.
- Tell your friends and ask them to share the link. If it's a site where they can "like" as well as "share," don't be afraid to ask people to help spread the word.
- Create a public page for your video and invite people to become fans. Each time you upload, update, or make a change, people you've already connected with will get the word.
- Existing websites, news sites, and TV sites are always looking for new uploads. Pick some that have a connection to your video. You could get your link on one of these sites, or even end up on TV.
- If you upload a better version later, you can delete the movie with all its comments, but first tell the fans of the original version.

BLOOPERS REEL

Maybe you shot funny mistakes, or the actors messing around? Edit all your goofy outtake scrap shots together to make a short "bloopers reel." Or, if you have just a few funny bloopers, put them at the end, after the credits roll. Or just show the bloopers to the cast and crew. You be the judge!

- Respond to nice comments. Ignore un-nice ones. Set your preferences to block comments, if you're feeling sensitive. But by all means, create a dialog with your audience. The more connected they feel, the more they'll like and share your link.

Upload to a social network media-sharing site

Each site has its own methods. It's easy, just learn by doing. Here's how most sites work.

- Log in to your account.
- Find and click the "share video" or "upload video" link.
- You'll get two choices:
    1. Record a webcam video.
    2. Upload a video file.
- Click the option to upload a video file.
- The following message will be displayed: "Select a video file on your computer."
- There will be some notes on screen that will tell you to only upload a video file if it is under the maximum file size or maximum number of minutes in length. Your video also needs to have been made by you or your friends. They don't want you to upload videos if you don't own the rights to the images or sound.
- Click the "browse" or "choose file" button to find your file.
- Enter text: title, comments, description, and keyword tags. The tags make it easier for people to search and find it. Here's where you assign privacy settings (like Public, Unlisted, and Private) to control comments.
- During the upload process, you'll see a progress bar. It may be *sloooooooow.*
- If you're feeling spontaneous, you can use the "record a webcam video" option to distribute a one-take video with no edits.

The Premiere

Premiere means "first," but it comes last. It's the moment you've been waiting for. Maybe you own a long red carpet. If you do, leave it where it is.

■ Where to stage it? A room with a big TV or video projector is a good start. If that TV is at someone else's house, your library, or your school, get permission first. Nobody likes hosting an unexpected screening.

■ Invitation list? Your crew, your cast, your friends, your family, and anyone who helped produce the film. Ask other kids from school to come see it, plus anyone who owns a lot of unpopped popcorn.

■ How to make it fun? Dress up in costumes or formal wear. Serve snacks. Decorate. Put photos of the actors on a piece of cardboard; write serious or funny captions. Maybe show your bloopers. After your movie, tell people

a couple of short, funny stories about what happened during the shoot. (And we mean *short*.) ALWAYS thank and give credit to your team. Being part of the fun is why they were there with you.

Promote

■ How to promote your movie premiere? Send e-mails. Make an online event page and invite your friends. Word of mouth. Hand out invitations to special guests. Put up posters only if it's cool. Invite a reporter from the school newspaper (or the local paper) to the shoot and to the premiere. Hire an advertising blimp (may be costly).

■ Post it on your social networking page or on other people's walls.

■ Send a request to your production team and other friends and family. Ask them to let their friends know about the premiere.

■ Issue a press release to your school paper, local papers, or event calendar.

Hey, you made it through the book. Even the editing part. That's a good start. Did you read every single word? Even the copyright information? Steven Spielberg would have. Or his little people, anyway.

Actually, you don't have to be Spike Lee or Spike Jonze to have fun making a video. You just have to learn some of the basics we covered between these covers, and practice them. And keep watching good movies – don't forget that part.

Whether you want to make real documentaries or fake films, music videos or talk shows, the tools and moves are the same. Just do your best, and you'll be amazed at the results. And you'll want to keep getting better.

Keep making movies

As we head off into the sunrise (we've been up all night writing), our publisher insists we say uplifting and support-ive things to you, in order to give you self-confidence or something like that. We think you're too savvy to fall for it, but hey, they run the show.

Congratulations, you star! You're on your way! We're proud of you! It's not so hard, really. And you'll just get better each time. Once you finish a movie, start another. Try something new each time. The basics will become much easier. Learning moviemaking is like learning a musical instrument. Practice! Experiment! Go for speed one time and quality the next. Learn bits about editing and you'll have a better idea of what to shoot. Experiment with animation, computer graphics, and sound effects to give yourself more ways to tell your story. Always tell a story. And keep having fun.

Can you believe some people do this for a living? It's true. Okay, they mainly stand on street corners with walkie-talkies, telling people they can't walk down their own street until the actors go home, but that's how you get paid in the biz while you make all your own independent movies on a shoestring budget. Are you feeling uplifted yet? See you at the movies.

~ Mark and Hazlitt

(who made their first video together in 1984)

There are a bunch of different types and versions and formats of movie scripts. Since this isn't a book about scriptwriting (or baking), we won't be discussing scripts (or fluffier pancakes). We've used one of the most common formats here. We've also scribbled in our shooting notes. Your script and notes can look different, and that's okay. We're cool with diversity. Do whatever is easiest for you.

Whether or not your movie is scary, writing and shooting from a script doesn't have to be.

The Incredible Killer Sweater from Outer Space

by

Mark N. Hazlitt

TITLE CARD 01:

The Incredible Killer Sweater from Outer Space

TITLE CARD 02:

A Video by Mark N. Hazlitt

TITLE CARD 03:

Somewhere in a city like yours …

FADE TO

SHOT 01: LS & tilt   EXTERIOR. BERNIE'S HOUSE – DAY

It's a beautiful day. All we see is bright blue sky, with some white, fluffy clouds. The camera tilts slowly down, past treetops, to the roof of a house in a quiet neighborhood. A UFO zips past the tilting camera. The camera stops when it is even with the front door of the house.

SPECIAL EFFECT: Frisbee attached to white shirt box

SHOT 02: CU   The UFO settles on the lawn as threatening music sounds.

SOUND EFFECT: scary music

SHOT 03: LS & dolly   We see the front of the house again. The camera dollies forward until the entire front door fills the frame. BERNIE, a skinny kid in baggy pants, opens the door and pokes his head out.

BERNIE:

SHOT 04: CU & tilt

(calling to someone in the house)
I'm sure I heard something. Maybe it was Little Jimmy teasing the cat again.

BETTY:

(off-screen)

You're hearing things. C'mon, deal the cards. You're losing.

Bernie closes the door. The camera tilts slowly from the door to a place under the bushes where the UFO is hiding. But the UFO's cargo pod is open ... and empty!

INTERIOR. LIVING ROOM – BERNIE'S HOUSE – SAME TIME

SHOT 05: MS

Bernie sits down at the table where he and BETTY are playing cards. Betty has most of the poker chips. Her small glasses magnify her cranky, concentrating eyes as she expertly deals a hand. Bernie is blowing on his cards, tapping them, knocking on wood. Then he looks at them and moans.

BERNIE:

Aargh! Aargh! Oh, ick!

BETTY:

OK, I bet 50 cents.

Bernie throws down his cards. At the same moment the cards hit the table, there is a loud CRASH!

SOUND EFFECT: giant explosion

BETTY:

Don't be a sore loser, Bernie.

SHOT 06: CU   Bernie's sweaty, nervous eyes widen.

BERNIE:

No, wait. That wasn't me this time. Honest.

SHOT 07: LS   Bernie gets up from the table. Betty hides her cards.

BERNIE:

(muttering)

Could it be?

BETTY:

Will you get me some fish sticks while you're out there, please?

SHOT 08: MS

INT. KITCHEN – BERNIE'S HOUSE – SAME TIME

A sweater flies through the air and lands on a chair with an ominous WHOOSH! As it settles, we hear footsteps approaching.

SOUND EFFECTS: ominous WHOOSH Footsteps

SHOT 09: LS

Bernie enters the kitchen.

BERNIE:

(to himself)

Now how did this sweater get over here?

Bernie picks up the sweater and pulls it on over his head as scary music builds.

SOUND EFFECT: scary music

SHOT 10: CU

The alien sweater monster tightens at the neck! Bernie struggles and clutches and grunts, then falls to the floor.

BERNIE:

Umph! Ugh! Argh! Oomf!

BETTY:

(off-screen)

Bernie! Will you stop eating all the fish sticks?

SHOT 11: CU

The sweater slowly peels itself off its victim, revealing Bernie's dead face.

BETTY:

(o.s.)

And don't stick your fingers in the tartar sauce, either!

SPECIAL EFFECT: unseen hand pulls sweater off-screen

SHOT 12: LS & pan

Bernie's body lies still as the sweater glides across the floor. The camera watches as the sweater creeps through the door and out of sight. We continue to watch the doorway as Betty talks from the room beyond.

BETTY:

(o.s.)

Oh, look, Bernie, the kitty is hiding in a sweater. Isn't that cute? I guess she's hiding from Little Jimmy. Here, kitty kitty, let me help you out of that turtleneck sweater.

SPECIAL EFFECT: unseen fishing line pulls sweater along

SHOT 13: LS & tilt

EXT. BERNIE'S HOUSE – SAME TIME

The house as we first saw it, but the neighborhood is not so quiet now …

BETTY:

(o.s.)

AAAAAAAHHHH!!!

The camera tilts up slowly back toward the sky.

FADE TO BLACK

GLOSSARY

analog video – A format that records video signals the traditional way. Any camera or VCR that isn't digital or DV is analog.

animatic – A series of still images with a soundtrack. Basically a storyboard on video with sound.

app – Short for software application.

aspect ratio – The size relationship between the width and the height of a screen. If your widescreen is 16:9 and it is 16 inches wide, then it is also 9 inches high. A football stadium screen might be 16 feet by 9 feet. The aspect ratio of a standard, more square screen is 4:3. Do the math.

auto-gain – An audio feature in cameras that sets the audio levels automatically. This can be great for having one less thing to worry about during your shooting, but pros set levels manually.

bloopers – A collection of outtakes with funny mistakes.

camcorder – Originally this meant a video camera with a built-in video cassette recorder. Now it generally means the same thing as "video camera." We almost always use the word camera in this book instead of camcorder, phone, webcam, etc.

cast – Everyone who appears on camera. Your group of actors. Casting is the action of choosing actors for your story.

clapperboard – That little hand-held chopper that gets clacked when the person says "Take one!" It helps you see which shot is which. It also connects sound and picture during the edit. Other names: clapper, clapboard, slate, slate board, sync slate, time slate, sticks, board, chopper (rare), finger guillotine (rarer), and marker.

clip – A digital video file or segment, usually cut from a longer shot.

compression – The practice of adjusting the sound levels on an audio track to make too-loud sounds quieter and too-quiet sounds louder.

concept – A plan, idea, or intention to make your movie.

coverage – Shooting more than you'll need so that when you get into editing, you don't need to go back and do a reshoot.

crew – Everyone who works on your movie behind the camera, as opposed to the cast.

cut – When you place two clips next to each other in the timeline without a transition in between. A.k.a. hard cut.

dailies – The *raw* (not edited) footage of a day's shoot. Watching them is a filmmaking tradition. See the mistakes so you can do better next time.

day-for-night – Shooting during the day, then applying post effects to darken the shots and give them a bluish tint, making it look like nighttime to the audience.

delegate – To give different people different jobs to do.

digital production – Any part of the process of making a movie where the video and audio signals are stored and edited in numerical form using computers.

digital video – A new format that records video the way computers read information – as data – without loss of quality.

dolly – (1) a toy human (2) to roll your camera toward or away from your subject on a wheeled platform. Dolly-in for moving closer, dolly-out for moving farther away.

ducking – A feature in some editing apps that will automatically mix the music lower when the actors are speaking.

final cut – The completed show when the director and producers agree to stop editing.

gaffer – The person in charge of rigging the lighting and power cords for the sets and taping down cords so nobody trips.

gaffer's tape – Duct tape, also known as duck tape. Gaffers use it for everything. Except fixing ducts, or ducks.

grip – The person on your production team in charge of adjusting sets, lighting, and props, and who sometimes assists the camera operator.

hard cut – See *cut*.

high def – High definition video; 720p is called HD and 1080p is called Full HD. See page 23 for details.

in the can – When a film is in the can, it's 100% finished. Because movies once were shipped to theaters in metal cans.

jump cut – When you cut between two shots of the same subject from slightly different camera angles.

limiter – An audio feature in cameras that keeps loud sounds from overloading your soundtrack during shooting.

location – Any place where you shoot video during your production.

low def – Low definition video. Everything below 720p is low def.

off-camera – Outside the field of view of your camera, and not recordable.

on-camera – Within the frame of the viewfinder of your camera, and recordable.

padding – Extra footage recorded at the beginning and/or ending of a shot. Allows extra room on the tape for editing.

pan – To swing your camera horizontally to give a panoramic effect or follow a subject.

pod – The authors made up this term. It comes from *tripod* and *monopod* (real words), both of which stabilize your camera. We describe many other ways to pod your camera!

post – Short for *post-production*, which means everything you do after shooting ends and before the final cut. This includes editing, titles, and computer-generated effects.

premiere – The first showing of your completed masterpiece. Usually there's a party.

pre-production – Everything you do to prepare before you start recording.

prop – Any visible item used by the actors is a prop.

range – Within a video clip, the *range* goes from the start point to the end point of the portion used in the edited video.

render – What a computer does when it converts all your video clips, effects, and edits into a single, complete movie file.

rough cut – The first edited version of your show. Usually it is a lot longer than the final cut, since there's always more editing (cutting) to do.

RTM – Read The Manual.

script – The written document containing the dialog, details about the action, and descriptions of camera shots, camera movements, sound effects, and music.

shoot – To record video. Or, the action of using the camera. Or, the name of what you're all working on together.

sound effects – Imitation sounds, such as of wind, thunder, or an explosion.

soundtrack – All the audio in a movie, including: music, dialog, sound effects. Sometimes refers to just the music, as in a soundtrack album.

storyboard – A series of drawings, typically with some written directions and dialog, showing the shots planned for your movie.

talent – A nice way to refer to your cast members. Say this with "air quotes" only if you wish to alienate them.

timeline – In your editing app, the graphical line of your video's titles, clips, and transitions.

trailer – A short promo for a longer movie. Used to run after (trail) the feature movie, but nowadays it runs before.

transition – Effect placed between two shots during editing, such as a dissolve, wipe, or fade.

tweak and twack – *Tweak* means "to adjust or fine-tune." We're not sure what *twack* means, but it sounds a lot like Elmer Fudd saying "track."

VCR – Video Cassette Recorder.

visual effects – Things done during the shoot to create illusions, such as of leaves falling, wind, or snow. Explosions and car crashes, too, but don't go there.

wrap party – A little bash you throw after the shooting to say thank you to the cast and crew for all their hard work, and to try to buy their silence regarding the true story of what happened off- camera. Sometimes you serve wraps, or burritos, but usually not.

zoom – A feature that lets you get closer to or farther from your subject without moving the camera. There are two types: 1) optical zoom, which moves lenses to zoom, yielding a high-quality image; 2) digital zoom, which uses the computer in your camera to select a smaller part of the digital video pickup chip (known as the CCD), yielding a lower-quality image.

INDEX

BROUGHT TO YOU BY...

Mark Shulman (co-author)

Mark Shulman writes for children and adults.

He was an early reader, an uncle at eight years old, a camp counselor, a radio newscaster, a New York City tour guide, and an advertising creative director before he started writing books. He is the youngest of five children, and he grew up with a Super 8 film camera. You got three minutes of film, couldn't erase any of it, had to mail your film to Kodak, send the equivalent of $30, and wait forever. After it came back, you had to edit with a razor blade and a bottle of glue, set up the noisy projector, turn out the lights, and then the projector light bulb would burn holes in your film. Mark loves video.

Mark graduated from East High School in Rochester, New York, and the University of Buffalo. His family lives in New York City, where his kids are filmed mercilessly. Find Mark at www.Shul.mn

Hazlitt Krog (co-author)

Hazlitt has worked as a producer of music, film, video, multimedia, animation, and websites for the past 25 years. His earliest memory is of playing with a Kodak Brownie camera under his crib. The youngest of four, he grew up an hour's drive due west of Mark.

Hazlitt got his first Super 8 movie camera, editing block, and projector at age 12 and was hooked. After graduating from Fredonia State University with a degree in Music, Video, and Film Production, his first job out of college was working on a Hollywood film called *The Natural*. He met Mark quite by accident on the phone. Soon after, they got together to make a boring training video about a humongous pump (for money), and they made a creative music video (for fun). They've since had many creative collaborations.

Hazlitt currently travels the world performing music and teaching the causes of happiness. He can be contacted at www.hazlitt.com.

Martha Newbigging (illustrator)

Martha Newbigging was lucky enough to grow up with two art teachers as parents. She started making animated films and flip books at the age of nine. She and her brother often hosted basement screenings for the neighborhood kids, showing their own cartoons along with films borrowed from the local library. She studied art and design at university and has illustrated more than a dozen children's books.